D0753627

Blacks in Political Office

Lucent Library of Black History

Other titles in this series:

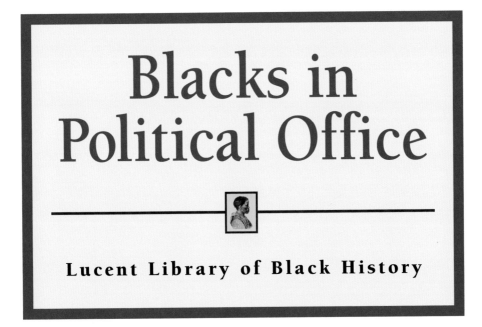

Blacks in Political Office

Lucent Library of Black History

Michael V. Uschan

LUCENT BOOKS

A part of Gale, Cengage Learning

GALE
CENGAGE Learning

Detroit • New York • San Francisco • New Haven, Conn • Waterville, Maine • London

GALE
CENGAGE Learning™

LIBRARY OF CONGRESS CATALOGING-IN-PUBLICATION DATA

Uschan, Michael V., 1948–
  Blacks in political office / by Michael V. Uschan.
    p. cm. — (Lucent library of Black history)
  Includes bibliographical references and index.
  ISBN 978-1-4205-0085-1 (hardcover)
  1. African American politicians—History. 2. African Americans—Politics
and government. 3. United States—Race relations. I. Title.
  E185.U76 2008
  320.973089'96073—dc22

                                                      2008017838

Lucent Books
27500 Drake Rd.
Farmington Hills, MI 48331

ISBN-13: 978-1-4205-0085-1
ISBN-10: 1-4205-0085-6

Printed in the United States of America
 2 3 4 5 6 7 12 11 10 09 08

Contents

Foreword

It has been more than 500 years since Africans were first brought to the New World in shackles, and over 140 years since slavery was formally abolished in the United States. Over 50 years have passed since the fallacy of "separate but equal" was obliterated in the American courts, and some 40 years since the watershed Civil Rights Act of 1965 guaranteed the rights and liberties of all Americans, especially those of color. Over time, these changes have become celebrated landmarks in American history. In the twenty-first century, African American men and women are politicians, judges, diplomats, professors, deans, doctors, artists, athletes, business owners, and home owners. For many, the scars of the past have melted away in the opportunities that have been found in contemporary society. Observers such as Peter N. Kirsanow, who sits on the U.S. Commission of Civil Rights, point to these accomplishments and conclude, "The growing black middle class may be viewed as proof that most of the civil rights battles have been won."

In spite of these legal victories, however, prejudice and inequality have persisted in American society. In 2003, African Americans comprised just 12 percent of the nation's population, yet accounted for 44 percent of its prison inmates and 24 percent of its poor. Racially motivated hate crimes continue to appear on the pages of major newspapers in many American cities. Furthermore, many African Americans still experience either overt or muted racism in their daily lives. A 1996 study undertaken by Professor Nancy Krieger of the Harvard School of Public Health, for example, found that 80 percent of the African American participants reported having experienced racial discrimination in one or more settings, including at work or school, applying for housing and medical care, from the police or in the courts, and on the street or in a public setting.

It is for these reasons that many believe the struggle for racial equality and justice is far from over. These episodes of discrimination threaten to shatter the illusion that America has completely overcome its racist past, causing many black Americans to become increasingly frustrated and confused. Scholar and writer Ellis Cose has described this splintered state in the following way: "I have done everything I was supposed to do. I have stayed out of trouble with the law, gone to the right schools, and worked myself nearly to death. What more do they want? Why in God's name won't they accept me as a full human being?" For Cose and others, the struggle for equality and justice has yet to be fully achieved.

In many subtle yet important ways the traumatic experiences of slavery and segregation continue to inform the way race is discussed and experienced in the twenty-first century. Indeed, it is possible that America will always grapple with the fallout from its distressing past. Ulric Haynes, dean of the Hofstra University School of Business has said, "Perhaps race will always matter, given the historical circumstances under which we came to this country." But studying this past and understanding how it contributes to present-day dialogues about race and history in America is a critical component of contemporary education. To this end, the Lucent Library of Black History offers a thorough look at the experiences that have shaped the black community and the American people as a whole. Annotated bibliographies provide readers with ideas for further research, while fully documented primary and secondary source quotations enhance the text. Each book in the series explores a different episode of black history; together they provide students with a wealth of information as well as launching points for further study and discussion.

Introduction

From Slavery to Public Office

On the evening of July 27, 2004, Barack Hussein Obama delivered the keynote address of the Democratic National Convention in Boston, Massachusetts. In a stirring speech to delegates and a national television audience of tens of millions of viewers, Obama explained that any greatness the United States had achieved was due to the guarantees of equality and liberty its founders made to all citizens in the Declaration of Independence. Obama said: "Our pride [in the nation] is based on a very simple premise, summed up in a declaration made over two hundred years ago, 'We hold these truths to be self-evident, that all men are created equal. That they are endowed by their Creator with certain inalienable rights. That among these are life, liberty and the pursuit of happiness.'"[1]

Obama said these powerful promises issued on July 4, 1776, had enabled him and millions of other African Americans to achieve great things despite the color of their skin. The son of an immigrant from Kenya who came to the United States to escape poverty in that African nation, Obama was able to attend college, become a lawyer, and be elected an Illinois state senator. Obama claimed, "I stand here knowing that my story is part of the larger American story [and] that, in no other country on earth, is my story even possible."[2]

Four months after Obama gave that dramatic speech, he won an election to become the fifth African American senator in U.S. history. He took office in January 2005 as one of thousands of black officials at every level of government. Whether they had been elected or appointed to their positions, they were all helping govern the powerful nation that had evolved from the struggling country that in 1776 had only just begun fighting to win its freedom from England in the American Revolution.

What Obama did not say in his speech, however, was that when Thomas Jefferson penned those promises, they were only meant for people with white skin. It would be almost another century before they would begin to become even partially true for blacks.

Slavery, Freedom, Political Power

In 1619 a Dutch ship landed in Virginia, the first of thirteen colonies England established in what was then called the New World. Aboard that ship were twenty Africans, the first blacks to arrive in the land that would one day become the United States of America. These first African Americans came not as passengers but cargo;

Senator Barack Obama speaks at the Democratic National Convention in 2004. For a first-term senator, it was a stunning accomplishment that, only four years later, he would be running for president of the United States.

they had been kidnapped from their homelands and transported to Virginia to be sold as slaves. For the next two centuries, hundreds of thousands of other Africans were brought to the United States and forced to live in slavery.

Even though the U.S. slave population would grow to 4 million by 1860, slavery divided the nation from its very beginning. Northern states opposed slavery and in 1787 tried to abolish it in the new U.S. Constitution. Southern states, which claimed they needed a source of cheap agricultural labor, defeated the attempt to end slavery. Tensions over slavery between North and South increased in the nineteenth century when northern states acted individually to abolish it. When Abraham Lincoln was elected president in 1860, the issue exploded into armed conflict. Eleven southern states were so sure Lincoln would end slavery that they seceded from the nation and formed the Confederate States of America. The Confederates began the Civil War on April 12, 1861, by bombing Fort Sumter, a Union military facility in Charleston, South Carolina.

The North won the Civil War, and the South's surrender on April 9, 1865, meant the end of slavery. During the Reconstruction era that followed the war, the Union army occupied southern states and forced them to give to blacks the rights the Constitution guaranteed its citizens. Frederick Douglass, a former slave who had escaped to the North before the war to become the nation's most influential black leader, believed the most important right blacks needed was the right to vote. He claimed that "slavery is not abolished until the black man has the ballot."[3]

Southern blacks began voting and electing officials, including many fellow African Americans. During Reconstruction two black U.S. senators, twenty U.S. representatives, and hundreds of state officials helped govern southern states in which they had once been slaves. This period of black political power, however, was short-lived. When federal officials withdrew the soldiers in 1876 to end Reconstruction, whites began taking civil liberties away from blacks, including their right to vote. When southern blacks became unable to vote, the number of southern black officials dwindled to a handful.

Black Power Grows Again

Even during Reconstruction, when hundreds of black officials served in the South, only a few lived anywhere else in the nation.

The reason was that so few blacks lived outside the South that they could not elect other blacks. But when black populations steadily increased in northern and western states during the first half of the twentieth century, they began electing black officials because they still had the right to vote there. For example, in 1918 Frederick Madison Roberts was elected to the California State Assembly, and in 1929 Oscar Stanton De Priest of Chicago became the first black elected to Congress from a northern state.

The vast majority of southern blacks were denied that right until Congress passed the Voting Rights Act of 1965. In the next few years the number of black elected officials nationwide exploded, rising from about 300 in 1964 to 1,469 in 1970. Most of the increase came in southern states, which had the largest black populations. However, more black officials were also elected elsewhere because of the rising number of black voters nationwide and a renewed interest among them to elect other blacks.

The number of black officials has steadily increased since then. In October 2007 the Joint Center for Political and Economic Studies reported the nation had more than ninety-five hundred black elected officials at all levels of government. Among them were Obama, Massachusetts governor Deval Patrick, and forty-two members of the U.S. House of Representatives. In 2007 there were also thousands of black officials who had been appointed to their positions, ranging from school district superintendents to U.S. secretary of state Condoleezza Rice.

Not Just Black but Competent

Although some black elected officials represent nearly all-black districts, many serve areas with mixed or predominantly non-black populations. One of them is Ronald Jones, who in 2007 was elected mayor of Garland, Texas. Ron Kirk, who in 1995 became the first black mayor of Dallas, said Jones's competence was more responsible for his election than the color of his skin. Said Kirk: "[Race] is relevant and it ought to be mentioned. But if you don't have the credentials and experience that people are looking for, it doesn't matter what color you are."[4] That competency, as well as the fact that blacks can vote after having been denied that right for so long during most of the nation's history, is why there are so many black officials today.

Chapter One

The First Black Political Officials

When the Civil War ended on April 9, 1865, the close of the conflict that nearly divided the nation forever ended slavery for nearly 4 million African Americans. But John Mercer Langston knew African Americans required more than their freedom to be able to lead decent lives. Langston believed he and other blacks needed the other rights white citizens had. In a speech in Indianapolis on October 25, 1865, Langston said that being able to vote was the most important right blacks needed:

> The colored man is not content when given simple emancipation. That certainly is his due but he demands much more than that: he demands absolute legal equality. [There] is one thing more, however, he demands; he demands it at the hands of the nation and in all the States. It is the free and untrammeled use of the ballot [and the] privilege of saying who shall make our laws, what they shall be, and who shall execute them.[5]

Langston spoke about that right from a unique vantage point. He had been elected to public office in two communities in Ohio even though he himself had never been allowed to vote because of the color of his skin. Langston was born free in 1829 in Louisa

County, Virginia, to plantation owner Ralph Quarles and Lucy Langston, an emancipated slave. After they died in 1834, Langston and his two brothers and one sister moved to Ohio, where slavery was illegal, to live with a family friend. The children inherited their father's wealth, which allowed Langston to attend Oberlin College. He graduated in 1849 and then studied for five more years to become Ohio's first black lawyer.

After Langston practiced law in Brownhelm, Ohio, for several years, the Liberty Party in March 1855 asked him to run for town

John Mercer Langston recognized that blacks had to have the right to vote to insure their equality with whites.

clerk. He won the election on April 2. After returning to Oberlin, Ohio, Langston served as a city councilman (1865–1867) and member of the city's Board of Education (1867–1868). He held those positions even though blacks could not vote.

Early Black Elected Officials

Langston was one of only a few African Americans who were elected before the Civil War, all of them in northern states where slavery was illegal. Alexander Lucius Twilight became the first black official in U.S. history on September 6, 1836, when he was elected to the Vermont General Assembly. Vermont was the first state to outlaw slavery—it did so in 1777—and was one of the few states that allowed blacks to vote before the war. Twilight was born on September 26, 1795, in Corinth, Vermont, to a free black father and a white mother. He attended Middlebury College in Vermont and in 1823 became the first African American to graduate from a U.S. college. Twilight was a teacher in Peru, New York, for several years before returning to Vermont, where he became principal of the Orleans County Grammar School in Brownington.

Twilight's legacy can still be seen today. He was instrumental in building a four-story, 60-foot-long (18m) granite building in Brownington known today as the Old Stone House Museum. In the 1830s Twilight designed and oversaw construction of the building as a student dormitory. Vermont historian Howard Frank Mosher claims little is known about the building. In a 1999 newspaper story, Mosher said, "To this day I don't think anyone really knows where he got the materials to build it, how much help he had, how long it took, even what inspired him to do it. He had a great vision."[6]

African American officials were a rarity until Reconstruction, the historical period that began after the Civil War and ran until 1877. During this brief period, hundreds of southern blacks were elected or appointed to positions ranging from sheriff to U.S. senator.

Reconstruction and "Interracial Democracy"

During Reconstruction, the federal government readmitted the eleven defeated southern states to the Union—Alabama, Arkansas, Florida, Georgia, Louisiana, Mississippi, North Carolina, South Carolina, Texas, Tennessee, and Virginia—and helped freed slaves

Reconstruction Helped Blacks

━━━━━━━━━━━━━━━━━━━■━━━━━━━━━━━━━━━━━━━

John Mercer Langston was free before the Civil War ended slavery, and he had even been a successful lawyer who became one of the nation's first black elected officials. But in a speech he delivered on May 17, 1874, in Oberlin, Ohio, Langston noted how much freedom and Reconstruction helped other African Americans:

> Within less than a quarter of a century, within the last fifteen years, the colored American has been raised from the condition of four footed beasts and creeping things to the level of enfranchised manhood. Within this period the slave oligarchy [rule] of the land has been overthrown, and the nation itself emancipated from its barbarous rule. [For] in the death of slavery, and through the change indicated, the colored American has been spoken into the new life of liberty and law [and] the moral atmosphere of the land is no longer that of slavery and hate; as far as the late slave, even, is concerned, it is largely that of freedom and fraternal appreciation.

John Mercer Langston, *Freedom and Citizenship: Selected Lectures and Addresses of Hon. John Mercer Langston, LL.D., U.S. Minister Resident at Haiti.* Miami: Mnemosyne, 1969, p. 142.

make new lives for themselves. The government forced southern states to adopt new constitutions that outlawed slavery and gave blacks equal rights with whites, including the right to vote. Federal officials also worked with the states to educate former slaves and find them homes and jobs.

Historian Eric Foner believes Reconstruction's most significant consequence was that black officials, many of them former slaves, helped govern the South. Foner claims, "[Reconstruction] was the first large-scale experiment in interracial democracy that had existed anywhere [in the world]."[7] This social and political experiment attracted northern journalists who were curious to see how blacks functioned as government officials. In 1873 *New York Times* reporter James Pike wrote favorably about black members of the South Carolina legislature: "Seven years ago these men were raising corn and cotton under the whip of an overseer. Today they are raising points of order and questions of privilege [in legislative debate]. They can raise one as well as the other. [Their new political power] means liberty. It means the destruction of prison walls only too real to them. It is the sunshine of their lives."[8]

Black officials were a novelty to northerners because there were few of them outside the South even during Reconstruction. Blacks throughout the nation had the right to vote, but not enough of them lived in other areas so they could elect fellow blacks to office, and most whites refused to vote for blacks. During this period in the South, however, black officials existed at every level of government.

Governing Their States

To be readmitted to the Union, southern states had to write new state constitutions. Hundreds of blacks helped perform that task, including Francis L. Cardozo, a delegate to the 1868 South Carolina Constitutional Convention. Cardozo was born free in Charleston, South Carolina. He was educated at the University of Glasgow in Scotland because southern states before the Civil War did not allow blacks to attend school.

Cardozo proposed a clause for the new constitution that ensured no one could ever take away the new freedom blacks had. Said Cardozo: "As colored men we have been cheated out of our rights for two centuries and now that we have the opportunity I want to fix them in the Constitution in such a way that no lawyer, however cunning, can possibly misinterpret the meaning."[9] Black delegates to constitutional conventions also proposed progressive ideas that benefited whites as well as blacks, such as free public schools.

After the federal government approved the new constitutions, the states held elections in which blacks could vote and run for office. About two thousand black officials were elected during Reconstruction. African Americans held local offices such as sheriff, tax collector, and judge, while others served as state legislators and congressmen.

This promising new political era for blacks, however, occurred even though many whites still did not consider blacks their equals. The main reason so many blacks were elected was that about 150,000 whites in the defeated states were barred from voting because during the Civil War they had been Confederate soldiers or government officials. That reduced the pool of eligible white voters in southern states to 635,000 compared to about 735,000 blacks. Five states even had more black voters than white voters—Mississippi, South

Blacks Were Fair to Whites

Joseph Hayne Rainey helped write the South Carolina constitution. On March 5, 1872, when he was a U.S. representative, Rainey gave a speech in which he said that he and other blacks had been fair to whites in creating the constitution:

> I ask the country, I ask white men, I ask Democrats, I ask Republicans whether the negroes have presumed to take improper advantage of the majority they [blacks] held in that State by disregarding the interest of the minority [whites]? They have not. Our convention which met in 1868, and in which the negroes were in a large majority, did not pass any proscriptive or disenfranchising acts, but adopted a liberal constitution, securing alike equal rights to all citizens white and black, male and female; as far as possible, mark you, we did not discriminate, although we had a majority. . . . You cannot show me one enactment by which the majority in our State have undertaken to [harm] the white men because the latter are in a minority.

Foster Rhea Dulles, *The United States Since 1865*. Ann Arbor: University of Michigan Press, 1971, p. 113.

Joseph Hayne Rainey helped write South Carolina's constitution.

A depiction of a meeting of the South Carolina legislature in 1873 reveals that many blacks participated in their local governments during Reconstruction.

Carolina, Louisiana, Alabama, and Florida. Still, some whites also voted for blacks because they supported the same political party, the Republican Party.

During Reconstruction, more than 630 blacks served in southern state legislatures. The first integrated state legislature in the nation's history met on April 2, 1870, when 8 blacks and 96 whites convened in Little Rock, Arkansas. When the South Carolina Legislature met in Columbia on July 6, 1870, it was the first with more black members (84) than white (72). James K. Green, a former slave who helped write Alabama's constitution, was a state legislator for eight years. Green said that he and other blacks joyously accepted their new government duties even though it was hard to do jobs they had never dreamed of doing before: "The tocsin [bell] of freedom sounded and knocked at the door and we walked out like free men and shouldered the responsibilities."[10]

Oscar J. Dunn on July 13, 1868, became the first of Louisiana's three African American lieutenant governors and the first black statewide elected official anywhere. Dunn was one of eighteen blacks during Reconstruction who served in state offices such as treasurer, superintendent of education, and secretary of state. A black even served as governor in Louisiana—P.B.S. (Pinckney Benton Stewart) Pinchback.

The First Black Governor

The first African American governor was born free in Macon, Georgia, on May 10, 1837. His parents were white plantation owner William Pinchback and Eliza Stewart, a freed slave. Pinchback attended school in Cincinnati until his father died in 1848. His white relatives rejected him and quit paying his tuition, which forced him to begin working. During the Civil War, Pinchback was a captain in the Union Army's 1st Louisiana Native Guards, and afterward he became active in politics. Pinchback was elected to the state senate in 1868 and was named to replace Dunn when the lieutenant governor died in 1871.

His opportunity to become governor came on December 9, 1872, when Louisiana governor Henry Clay Warmoth was removed from office. Warmoth was impeached for illegal activities during the 1872 gubernatorial election won by William P. Kellogg. Pinchback became acting governor until Kellogg was sworn in as governor on January 13, 1873. Pinchback performed ably in his short tenure despite threats of violence by whites who did not think a black should hold such a powerful position. When Pinchback requested a federal ruling about his right to be governor, U.S. attorney general George H. Williams assured him, "You are recognized by the President as the lawful executive of Louisiana."[11] Williams also sent troops to protect Pinchback from racist whites.

On the day Kellogg was inaugurated, Pinchback said he was giving up the office "with the hope that your administration will be as fair toward the class that I specially represent [blacks] as mine has been to the class that you represent [whites]."[12] The next day, the state senate elected Pinchback to the U.S. Senate. State legislatures chose senators until 1913, when the U.S. Constitution was changed to let voters choose them. Pinchback had also been elected to Congress by voters in the election that made Kellogg governor, and Pinchback is the only person ever elected to both houses of Congress at the same time.

Pinckney Pinchback served as an interim governor in the state of Louisiana and was elected senator by the Louisiana legislature in 1872.

Blacks Go to Congress

Despite his twin victories, Pinchback never served in Congress because his Democratic opponents claimed he had won through voting irregularities. The Senate and House have the power to settle such disputes before seating new members, and both legislative bodies ruled against Pinchback. Another African American who suffered a similar fate was John Willis Menard of Louisiana, who on November 3, 1868, was the first black elected to Congress. On February 23, 1869, Menard became the first black to speak before the U.S. House of Representatives when he asked it to declare him the winner in his disputed election. The House rejected him because of white members such as future president James A. Garfield of Ohio, who claimed that it was "too early to admit a Negro to the U.S. Congress."[13] It was not until December 12, 1870, that Joseph Hayne Rainey of South Carolina became the first black to be both elected and accepted by the House as a member of Congress.

Twenty African Americans served in the House of Representatives during Reconstruction. Although thirteen had been slaves, most were well educated. Rainey, who was born a slave in 1832 in Georgetown, South Carolina, was reelected to Congress four times and was a member of Congress longer than any other black during Reconstruction. Rainey was an eloquent speaker and in April 1871 delivered a stirring speech to support a House bill to protect southern blacks from the Ku Klux Klan, a racist group that used violence to deny blacks their rights. His speech helped win passage of the bill.

Rainey, however, was not the first black to sit in Congress. On February 25, 1870, Hiram Rhodes Revels of Mississippi was sworn in as the first black U.S. senator. An African Methodist Episcopal minister, he served as a chaplain for black soldiers during the Civil War. Following the war he went into politics. In January 1870 the Mississippi senate elected Revels 81–15 to fill the unexpired U.S. Senate term of Jefferson Davis, who had quit the Senate when he became president of the Confederate States of America.

Revels became a senator after the Senate debated for three days on whether to accept him. Several southern senators argued that an African American was not worthy of joining the nation's most powerful legislative body. Among them was Senator Garrett Davis

Senator Blanche Kelso Bruce rose from slavery to become the first black man to serve a full Senate term, elected in Mississippi in 1874. He also started the first elementary school for black children.

of Kentucky, who claimed, "This is certainly a morbid state of affairs. Never before in the history of this government has a colored been elected to the Senate."[14] Other senators refused to accept that racist argument. Revels served until March 3, 1871, to complete Davis's term.

The first black to serve a full Senate term was Blanche Kelso Bruce, who was elected on February 3, 1874, by the Mississippi senate. Born a slave on March 1, 1841, in Farmville, Virginia, he and his two brothers escaped to Missouri in 1861. Bruce, whose owner had allowed him to be educated, began Missouri's first elementary school for blacks, and in 1869 he moved to Mississippi. Two years later he was appointed a tax assessor, and the next year he was elected sheriff. After Bruce helped Adelbert Ames win election as Mississippi's governor by getting blacks to vote for him, the state senate, which Ames controlled, rewarded Bruce by electing him to the U.S. Senate.

Bruce fought racial discrimination against blacks and others, including Chinese immigrants and Native Americans. One of his major accomplishments was chairing a committee that investigated the failure of a federal bank; he helped uncover massive fraud and was able to return savings to sixty-one thousand depositors. He made history on February 14, 1879, when he presided over

A Nervous Black Congressman

Robert Brown Elliott was a U.S. representative from South Carolina from 1871 to 1874. Although Elliott was considered a brilliant speaker, he admitted in a story in the *New National Era* newspaper on March 19, 1874, how nervous he was the first time he spoke in the House of Representatives:

> I shall never forget that day, when rising in my place to address the House, I found myself the center of attention. Everything was still. Those who believed in the natural inferiority of the colored race appeared to feel that the hour had arrived in which they should exult in triumph over the failure of the man of "the despised race" whose voice was about to be lifted in that chamber. The countenances of those who sympathized with our cause seemed to indicate their anxiety for my success, and their heart-felt desire that I might prove equal to the emergency. I cannot picture to you the emotions that then filled my mind.

Dorothy Sterling, ed., *The Trouble They Seen: Black People Tell the Story of Reconstruction*. New York: Doubleday, 1976, p. 178.

the Senate in the absence of vice president William A. Wheeler. The *New York Tribune* newspaper reported, "This is the first time a colored man ever sat in the seat of the Vice President of the United States. Senator Bruce is universally respected by his fellow senators and is qualified both in manners and character to preside over the deliberations of the most august body of men in the land."[15]

Black Officials Served Well

It was not unusual in this period for black congressmen to be praised by newspapers and even their white colleagues. U.S. senator James G. Blaine once said, "The colored men who took their seats in both the Senate and House were as a rule studious, earnest, ambitious men, whose public conduct would be honorable to any race."[16]

Black officials who earned such praise included Civil War hero Robert Smalls. Smalls was born a slave in Beaufort, South Carolina, but learned to pilot ships. During the war, the Confederates forced him to pilot the *Planter*. On May 12, 1862, while the *Planter*'s officers were ashore, Smalls sailed the ship out of Charleston's harbor and gave it to Union ships blockading the South Carolina port. Smalls, his wife and children, and several other blacks escaped slavery in the daring move.

After piloting Union ships during the war, Smalls served in the South Carolina legislature and Congress. He was also U.S. collector of customs in Beaufort for nearly two decades. Smalls once wrote that he tried to do a good job because he knew his work would reflect on other blacks: "During the twenty years I have held the position of Collector, I have succeeded to so manage affairs that when I leave it, I will do so with credit to myself, my family, and my race."[17]

Chapter Two

Blacks Lose, Then Regain, Political Power

During Reconstruction hundreds of African Americans were elected officials in southern states. This happened despite the opposition of many southern whites who believed blacks were inferior and should not be able to hold office or even vote. This racist belief was summed up by South Carolina governor Benjamin Perry, who shortly after the Civil War ended in 1865 claimed, "This is a white man's government and intended for white men only."[18] During Reconstruction, however, South Carolina had many African American officials.

Blacks were able to enjoy such political power during this historic period in U.S. history despite white hatred, because Congress had placed the South under military rule. Congress even stationed nearly forty thousand soldiers in the South to keep the defeated southern states from denying blacks their constitutional rights. However, even the might of the U.S. Army could not make whites willingly accept blacks as their equals or completely stop them from brutalizing African Americans who dared to exercise those rights.

White Violence Against Blacks

Southern whites who opposed black equality after the Civil War joined the Ku Klux Klan (KKK), the White League, and the Knights of the White Camellia. These racist groups terrorized blacks to make them so afraid of whites that they would not dare to exercise rights they now had, such as voting, attending school, or owning land. Confederate general Nathan Bedford Forrest joined the KKK in 1866 because he believed that it could, "keep the niggers in their place."[19] Forrest was the Klan's first Grand Wizard, its top official.

Ku Klux Klansmen terrorize a black man in North Carolina in 1871. Whites joined such groups to keep blacks from exercising their rights, especially the right to vote.

Much of the violence during Reconstruction was aimed at stopping blacks from voting. Whites knew that the key to blacks winning equality with whites was to have the power to elect officials who would treat them fairly. Whites physically attacked blacks who tried to vote or were themselves elected. For example, in 1868 in Camilla, Georgia, a mob killed more than twenty African Americans at a Republican rally because they feared the blacks would vote for that party's candidates. And on April 13, 1873, a large group of whites murdered seventy blacks in Colfax, Louisiana, in a dispute over which candidates had been elected in November 1872. When elected African American officials, including Sheriff R.C. Register, tried to take office, whites used guns and a cannon to kill several of them. The mob then went on a rampage throughout Colfax, destroying black homes and businesses and killing many more blacks in Reconstruction's bloodiest race riot.

During Reconstruction whites threatened or assaulted about 10 percent of black officials. Abram Colby was beaten on October 29, 1869, by whites who were upset he had been elected a Georgia state legislator. "They broke my door open," he said, "took me out of bed, took me to the woods, and [whipped] me three hours or more and left me for dead."[20] Andrew J. Flowers was whipped after being elected justice of the peace in Tennessee. He said Klan members told him they did it "because I had the impudence to run against a white man for office, and beat him. They said that they did not intend any nigger to hold office in the United States."[21] Both survived the beatings, but whites murdered at least thirty-five black officials in similar attacks.

Despite such violence, hundreds of thousands of blacks voted in this period and about two thousand were elected. This brief heyday of black political power, however, ended in 1877 because of a political deal between the Democratic and Republican parties that ended Reconstruction.

The End of Reconstruction

The new rights and the protection blacks enjoyed during Reconstruction were due to white Republicans who controlled the majority of votes in Congress and held the presidency. Republicans like Senator Charles Sumner of Massachusetts believed blacks deserved equal rights, especially the power to vote. "This is the great guarantee," Sumner said of voting, "without which all other guarantees fail."[22] Although the Republicans had used their political power to impose Reconstruction on the South to help blacks, they also had a political motive for creating Reconstruction. The Republicans also wanted to make sure that they continued to be stronger nationally than the Democratic Party.

The Democratic Party had always been dominant in the South because it had always supported slavery. When blacks began voting, they always voted Republican because that party had ended slavery and given them their new rights. Black votes strengthened the Republicans in southern states, as did the fact that hundreds of thousands of whites who were Democrats were not allowed to vote for several years as punishment for waging the Civil War. Those two factors helped the Republican Party win southern states so it could elect Republican Ulysses S. Grant president in 1868 and 1872.

Republican political power began to fade in the mid-1870s as new western states began voting Democrat. The Democrats also grew stronger in southern states when tens of thousands of former Confederate soldiers and officials became eligible again to vote. By 1876 only Florida, Louisiana, and South Carolina still had Republican-controlled governments.

This situation created a political crisis in the 1876 presidential election between Democrat Samuel Tilden and Republican Rutherford B. Hayes. When both parties claimed victory in Florida, Louisiana, and South Carolina, an electoral commission composed of Democrats and Republicans was created to settle the dispute because the electoral votes from those three states would decide the election.

The commission awarded the states to Hayes, giving him 185 electoral votes, one more than Tilden. The decision, however, was based on a political compromise between the two parties and not actual vote totals. The Republicans wanted to retain the presidency so much that they made a deal with the Democrats. The Republicans said that if the commission gave the votes to Hayes so he could become president, Hayes would end Reconstruction and allow whites to govern southern states without any interference from the federal government. The two parties agreed to the compromise, and Hayes was sworn in as president on March 2, 1877.

An illustration depicts members of Congress recounting the electoral vote after the contested Tilden-Hayes election. In reality, a behind-the-scenes deal between the Republicans and Democrats allowed Hayes to win the election.

Hayes defended the political compromise, saying he was sure that "absolute justice and fair play to the negro [was possible] by trusting the honorable and influential [southern] whites."[23] *Nation* magazine, however, claimed the deal meant that "the negro will disappear from the field of national politics."[24] The magazine believed that southern whites would take political power away from blacks, and its prediction was the one that came true.

Southern Blacks Lose Their Rights

In South Carolina, Democratic governor Wade Hampton ordered attorney general Robert Brown Elliott and other black officials to quit. In a letter to Hampton, Elliott said he realized Hampton could force him to leave but noted that the dismissal "will obviously [deny Elliott] rights guaranteed by that Constitution which he [Hampton] has sworn to obey."[25] Elliott was referring to the state's constitution, which he had helped write. Elliott had to comply with the demand two weeks later after the state supreme court sided with Hampton. The court's white justices knew Elliott had been legally elected but allowed Hampton to remove him because they also did not want blacks serving as officials. The federal government refused to do anything to stop this injustice.

Southern states in the next two decades changed their constitutions and passed new laws to deny blacks the right to vote. When Reconstruction ended in 1877 Robert Toombs of Georgia, a former U.S. senator and Confederate general, said, "Give us a convention, and I will fix it so that the [white] people shall rule and the Negro shall never be heard from."[26] Toombs helped draft a constitution that included a poll tax people had to pay before they could vote; many blacks were so poor they could not afford it. Other measures to bar black voters included party primary elections restricted to white voters and literacy tests, which many blacks could not pass because they had never gone to school.

The federal government failed to stop southern states from denying blacks those rights, even though the United States during Reconstruction had approved three amendments to the U.S. Constitution that guaranteed blacks such rights. The Thirteenth Amendment abolished slavery, the Fourteenth Amendment made African Americans citizens, and the Fifteenth Amendment prohibited denying any citizen the right to vote due to race, color, or previous condition of servitude. Congress had the power to enforce the amendments, but it refused to do anything for nearly a century because it was indifferent to the plight of blacks.

Whites continued to use violence to deny blacks their rights. They attacked individual blacks who dared to vote and also conducted large-scale episodes of racial violence. The worst incident occurred in Wilmington, North Carolina, on November 10, 1898, when a mob of two thousand whites led by Alfred Moore Waddell took control of the port city and forced black and white Republican officials to resign. Even though at least twenty-two African Americans were killed in the brutal takeover of Wilmington's government, neither state nor federal officials punished anyone. In a book on the bloody incident, David S. Cecelski and Timothy B. Tyson write that the violence was not a race riot but a political insurrection: "In its overall effect [the] event was nothing less than a revolution against interracial democracy."[27]

By 1900 the cumulative effect of discriminatory state laws, white intimidation, and federal indifference reduced the number of black voters to only about 3 percent of eligible southern blacks. The small number of black voters meant that black office holders became a rarity in the South for nearly a century.

Black Officials Outside the South

The scarcity of black voters also affected black representation in Congress. U.S. representative George Henry White, the last former slave to serve in Congress, was elected in 1896 and 1898 from his native North Carolina. The state had a sizable number of black voters until 1900, when its legislature passed literacy and poll tax

Violence in Wilmington

━━━━━━━━━━━■━━━━━━━━━━━

The Reverend J. Allen Kirk, a black minister, witnessed the riot in Wilmington, North Carolina, on November 10, 1898, in which whites took control of the city's government and murdered at least twenty-two blacks. Kirk describes the violence he saw:

> The colored people [were] all exposed to death. Firing began, and it seemed like a mighty battle in war time. The shrieks and screams of children, of mothers, of wives were heard, such as caused the blood of the most inhuman person to creep. Thousands of women, children and men rushed to the swamps and there lay upon the earth in the cold to freeze and starve. The woods were filled with colored people. The streets were dotted with their dead bodies. [Some] bodies were left lying in the streets until the next day following the riot. Some were found by the stench and miasma that came forth from their decaying bodies under their houses.

J. Allen Kirk, "A Statement of Facts Concerning the Bloody Riot in Wilmington, N.C. Of Interest to Every Citizen of the United States," in University of North Carolina at Chapel Hill, *Documenting the American South*. http://docsouth.unc.edu/nc/kirk/kirk.html.

measures that restricted the number of black voters. As a result, White was defeated in 1900, and by 1910 black voting in North Carolina had been almost entirely eliminated. Another black congressman would not be elected until 1928, when Oscar Stanton De Priest of Illinois became the first African American elected to Congress from a northern state. De Priest's election symbolized a significant shift in the history of black elected officials.

The Reconstruction period was the first time large numbers of blacks held office, but that occurred only in the South because so few African Americans lived in other states. This situation started changing after Reconstruction when blacks began leaving the South. They moved to northern and western states because southern whites denied them their rights and employed violence to keep them submissive; nearly 90 percent of the 3,445 black

A Dream of Black Independence

In 1890 Edward P. McCabe established the African American community of Langston City in the Oklahoma Territory. Although it never happened, McCabe predicted in an October 23, 1891, newspaper article in the *American Citizen* that so many blacks would move to Oklahoma that they would be able to govern it. McCabe said:

> [In Oklahoma] the negro can rest from mob law, here he can be secure from every ill of the southern policies. . . . I expect to have a Negro population of over one hundred thousand [in Oklahoma] within two years [and] we will by that time secure control of political affairs. [The] time will soon come when we will be able to dictate the policy of this territory or state, and when that time comes we will have a Negro state governed by Negroes. We do not wish to antagonize the whites. They are necessary in the development of a new country, but they owe my race homes, and my race owes to itself a governmental control of those homes.

Martin Dunn, "From Sodom to the Promised Land: E.P. McCabe and the Movement for Oklahoma Colonization," *Kansas Historical Quarterly*, Autumn 1974, p. 376.

An African American family stands outside their makeshift shack in Oklahoma in 1889. Many African Americans relocated to Oklahoma in the hopes of establishing a state where they had political power.

people lynched in the United States between 1882 and 1968 were murdered in the South.

The first wave of blacks to leave were called Exodusters; their name derives from Exodus, the biblical account of how the Israelites fled slavery in Egypt. In 1879 and 1880 as many as forty thousand blacks left Mississippi and Louisiana for Kansas, which had opposed slavery before the Civil War. Edward P. McCabe, who had been born free in Troy, New York, also moved to Kansas so he could help blacks start new towns. McCabe became a leading Republican Party official and in 1882 and 1884 was elected state auditor. McCabe a few years later joined thousands of blacks who migrated to the Oklahoma Territory, an area he claimed was free of racial discrimination: "Here the negro can rest from mob law, here he can be secure from every ill of the southern policies."[28] On October 22, 1890, McCabe founded Langston City, which he named after John Mercer Langston, an early black official in Ohio. McCabe from 1897 until 1907 was deputy auditor of the Oklahoma Territory. Blacks were able to create communities in such unpopulated western areas because nobody was there to bother them.

Between 1890 and 1920, in what was known as the Great Migration, about nine hundred thousand blacks left the South for big northern cities like New York, Chicago, Pittsburgh, and Cleveland. They moved in search of better jobs and to escape segregation and discrimination. The pace of this historic migration peaked during World War I, when an estimated five hundred thousand blacks headed north. This population shift enabled the election of black officials. De Priest, for example, was elected to the Cook County board in 1904. But as Chicago blacks grew in political strength, De Priest was elected to ever more powerful positions; he became the city's first black alderman in 1915 and then a congressman. This pattern of black migration and political growth repeated itself in many other cities.

Few, if any, black officials were elected in the South in the first half of the twentieth century because whites did not let blacks vote. A rarity was Charles W. Anderson, who in 1936 won a seat in the Kentucky General Assembly to become the first southern black state legislator since Reconstruction. That unjust situation did not change until blacks won back their civil rights in the 1960s.

The Second Reconstruction

The civil rights struggle that finally ended such discrimination began in 1956, when blacks in Montgomery, Alabama, led by the Reverend Martin Luther King Jr., began a protest that erased a law that forced blacks to sit in the rear of buses and give up their seats to whites. That small but important victory soon ignited other protests in the South to allow blacks to eat in restaurants, shop in stores, and stay in hotels that were reserved for whites. In the 1960s this historic battle began to focus on the right to vote.

The largest civil rights rally of this turbulent era occurred on August 28, 1963, in Washington, D.C. The most memorable speech that day was delivered by King, who told 250,000 people he had a dream that whites and blacks would one day live in harmony. King said a key element to realizing that dream was the right of blacks to vote: "We cannot be satisfied as long as a Negro in Mississippi cannot vote and a Negro in New York believes he

President Johnson and the Voting Rights Act

On March 15, 1965, President Lyndon B. Johnson addressed Congress to ask it to pass the Voting Rights Act of 1965. Johnson said:

I speak tonight for the dignity of man and the destiny of democracy. I urge every member of both parties, Americans of all religions and of all colors, from every section of this country, to join me in that cause. . . . We cannot, we must not, refuse to protect the right of every American to vote in every election that he may desire to participate in. And we ought not, and we cannot, and we must not wait [any longer] before we get a bill. We have already waited a hundred years and more, and the time for waiting is gone. [The] time of justice has now come. I tell you that I believe sincerely that no force can hold it back. It is right in the eyes of man and God that it should come. And when it does, I think that day will brighten the lives of every American.

Lyndon Baines Johnson, "We Shall Overcome," speech delivered to a Joint Session of Congress on March 15, 1965. www.americanrhetoric.com/speeches/lbjweshallovercome.html.

has nothing for which to vote. No, no, we are not satisfied, and we will not be satisfied until justice rolls down like waters, and righteousness like a mighty stream."[29]

The struggle for the ballot was violent because whites knew black political power was the key to their gaining equality. Whites brutally beat blacks who tried to register to vote and murdered blacks and whites who led drives to register black voters. This racial hatred was displayed in Selma, Alabama, on March 7, 1965, a day that became known as "Bloody Sunday." When six hundred blacks marched for the right to vote, state troopers and Dallas County sheriff's deputies stopped them from crossing the Edmund Pettus Bridge so they could not continue marching to Montgomery, Alabama's capital. Law enforcement officials fired tear gas at protesters, some of them young children, and beat them with whips, billy clubs, and chains. Seventy blacks were wounded, one person died, and televised news reports shocked the nation and the world.

One week later on March 15, President Lyndon B. Johnson addressed Congress. Declaring, "Every American citizen must have an equal right to vote,"[30] Johnson proposed the Voting Rights Act of 1965. The law reaffirmed the right blacks had to vote and, more important, provided federal enforcement to ensure they could exercise that right. Attempts by southern congressmen to kill the bill delayed its passage, but Johnson finally signed it into law on August 6.

Chapter Three

Blacks Govern Their Hometowns

The new political power blacks won from their dramatic victories in the civil rights struggles of the 1960s quickly began to change the nation. The Joint Center for Political and Economic Studies has tracked the growth of black elected officials since 1970. In its initial report in 1970, the group said the United States had 1,469 black elected officials, which was more than four times the 300 black officials in 1964. Thomas E. Cavanagh and Denise Stockton authored the report. They said that the Voting Rights Act made the huge change possible: "The 1960s witnessed the most dramatic political progress by the black community in American History. By the end of the decade, black mayors and congressmen had become visible symbols of the capacity of the American political system to respond to minority aspirations at the polls."[31]

By 2000 the number of black elected officials in the United States had grown to 9,040. Thousands of them were governing their hometowns as mayors and members of city and town councils, county boards, and school boards. There were nearly five hundred black mayors throughout the nation, including Lee Brown (Houston), Dennis Archer (Detroit), Wellington E. Webb (Denver), and Willie L. Brown Jr. (San Francisco). Another was

James Perkins Jr., mayor of Selma, Alabama, the scene of one of the most dramatic civil rights battles.

Electoral Justice for Selma

As a twelve-year-old, Perkins, on March 7, 1965, had witnessed "Bloody Sunday" in Selma, even though he had to defy his parents to do it. Although Perkins had participated in other protests for black rights, his parents would not let him march because they feared violence. "I cried and cried," Perkins said, "but they said no." Perkins went anyway after the march began, and what he saw shocked him: "I ran out the back door [of the family home] and down to Brown Chapel church, where the marchers were reconvening. I saw them, tear gas in their eyes, beaten up [by law officers]."[32]

Selma mayor Joe Smitherman had done nothing to stop the brutal attacks because blacks could not vote him out of office. When Smitherman was elected in 1964, Selma had only 150 registered black voters even though thousands of African Americans lived there. Blacks marched that day because they were an-

Alabama state troopers patrol amid a fog of tear gas during "Bloody Sunday" in Selma. Such violence propelled Congress to pass the Voting Right Acts of 1965.

gry they had no say in electing officials like Smitherman. Even though "Bloody Sunday" helped persuade Congress to pass the Voting Rights Act of 1965, Smitherman remained mayor for the next thirty-five years. Perkins, the young boy who had been horrified by the violence he saw, was the candidate who finally beat Smitherman on September 12, 2000. "They always said, 'Joe gotta go,' and now Joe gone,"[33] Smitherman said in conceding defeat. Perkins, by then a forty-seven-year-old computer consultant, won with 57 percent of a record eleven thousand votes cast.

Historian Frank Sikora believes Perkins's victory was important even though there had been black mayors in southern cities for several decades: "Blacks have won offices across the South, but none is as important a symbol as this one."[34] Perkins's victory was significant because blacks across the county still considered Selma a symbol of the racism that had denied them their rights for so long.

His election was a gratifying reminder of how much black political power had grown since 1965. And it was in southern communities, where blacks had once been subjected to such brutal treatment, that black officials were able to make the biggest improvements in the lives of other blacks.

Black Mayors in the South

One of the nation's first black mayors was Charles Evers, who on May 13, 1969, defeated R.J. "Turnip Green" Allen 433-264 in Fayette, Mississippi, a small, racially mixed town of seventeen hundred people. When Evers became Mississippi's first black mayor in nearly a century, he said, "I hope white people and black people, particularly in Mississippi, understand that we've only done the thing that God wanted us to do—to take part in our government and make it work for everybody."[35] His election was significant because his brother, Medgar Evers, had been shot to death on June 12, 1963, by a white supremacist in Jackson, Mississippi, for leading the fight in Mississippi for black rights.

Evers was elected because the Voting Rights Act of 1965 freed black political power in the South, where the large numbers of blacks helped to begin electing mayors and other local officials. He was not, however, the first southern black mayor. On May 6, 1969, Howard Lee was elected in Chapel Hill, North Carolina, to

Charles Evers became the first black mayor of a small town in Mississippi in 1969. Such victories were largely due to the Voting Right Acts of 1965.

become the first southern mayor since Reconstruction. Lee won by 400 votes out of a record 4,734 cast by voters in a community that was only 10 percent black. After his narrow victory, Lee admitted he worried about people "both black and white, who constantly wonder whether a black man is really capable of handling the reins of municipal government."[36] But Lee did such a good job, including bringing about a reliable new bus system, that he was overwhelmingly elected to two more terms.

The first black mayor of a southern city with fifty thousand or more residents was Atlanta's Maynard Jackson Jr., who was elected in 1974 and served three terms. Jackson hired more blacks for city jobs and pressured local businesses to increase African American employment. Jackson also improved city transportation and transformed Hartsfield Atlanta International Airport into one of the nation's most modern airports. Atlanta has had a black mayor ever since Jackson won, earning it the nickname "Blacklanta."

Many other blacks have since headed southern cities. In 1978 Ernest "Dutch" Morial was elected mayor of New Orleans (his son Marc Morial became the city's mayor in 1994); in 2007 Bernard Kincaid became mayor of Birmingham, Alabama, the scene of bitter racial violence during the civil rights struggles of the 1960s; and in 1991 Willie Herenton was chosen mayor of Memphis, Tennessee. When Herenton was reelected for a third term on October 7, 1999, his top opponent was also black—city council chairman Joe Ford. Even though a majority of voters in Memphis were black, Herenton in his victory speech stressed that the city "must have a spirit of unity that crosses race, politics and economics [to] move forward."[37]

Working with whites was important to black mayors in cities with large black populations. It was even more vital in cities outside that region in which white voters were in the majority.

The First Black Mayors

No one was surprised when southern blacks began electing local officials, because there were so many black voters. However, the nation's first black mayors came to power in cities in northern and western states. Racism in those areas of the nation was not as strong as it was in the South, which made it more acceptable for whites to vote for blacks.

Robert C. Henry became the nation's first post-Reconstruction mayor in January 1966 when the Springfield (Ohio) City Commission appointed him to the position. The office of mayor in Springfield, which was mostly white, was an honorary position that by tradition went to the commissioner who received the most

Wooing White Voters

Carl B. Stokes needed white votes to become Cleveland's mayor. The city had several large groups of immigrants from Europe. In *Contemporary Black Leaders*, historian Elton C. Fox describes how Stokes met with many of them to get their support, including editors of the newspapers they read:

> He began by having a breakfast meeting with the editors of the foreign language newspapers read by those Clevelandites with roots in Eastern Europe. On the following day he was editorially endorsed on the front page of the Hungarian daily, *Szabadsag*. The daily declared that under Stokes's leadership, "all of us could live up to the ideals that inspired the ethnic groups to settle in Cleveland in their search for freedom and in the pursuit of happiness." Candidate Stokes did not fail to tell those "ethnic" whites of his own poverty, of his mother's struggles. He said, "My mother raised me and my brother with the argument that if you study hard, you've got to become somebody. *I know every European immigrant parent told his children the same thing!*"

> Elton C. Fox, *Contemporary Black Leaders*. New York: Dodd, Mead, 1970, pp. 160–61.

Carl Stokes appealed to the city's immigrant voters to become mayor of Cleveland.

votes in the last election. Henry, a commissioner since 1962, had topped all commissioners in the November 1965 election. The *Springfield Sun* newspaper had backed his reelection, claiming that he "began public service as Springfield's first Negro city commissioner and long since proved himself everyone's commissioner."[38] Thomas R. Yarborough also benefited from the support of white voters in 1966 when he was elected mayor in Lake Elsinore, California.

However, political scientists David R. Colburn and Jeffrey S. Adler cite November 7, 1967, as the day in which African Americans truly began to win political power in U.S. cities. On that historic day, Carl B. Stokes in Cleveland and Richard G. Hatcher in Gary, Indiana, were both elected mayor of large cities. Stokes realized how big an accomplishment it was for him to defeat Seth Taft. He knew that the victory of the grandson of a slave over the grandson of a former U.S. president—William Howard Taft—signaled a new era of African American political power: "There is a certain kind of winning that is more than a victory, it is a release. A man plays the numbers [lottery] for years, every day the same number, and every day losing. [One] day the number comes in and he is set free. Set free."[39] Colburn and Adler claim the victories were important because they "changed American urban and political history. After three and one-half centuries of complete or relative disfranchisement [being unable to vote], African Americans [began seizing] the mayor's office in nearly every major city in the nation."[40] Within a decade of the victories two hundred African American mayors were elected, and by 1990 black mayors had headed the nation's three largest cities—Thomas Bradley in Los Angeles (1973), Harold Washington in Chicago (1983), and David Dinkins in New York (1990).

The early black victories outside the South surprised political analysts. Even though blacks living there had been able to vote since Reconstruction, they had often been lax in exercising that right. However, the struggle of southern blacks to vote ignited a new passion for political activity in blacks around the nation. That new attitude was coupled with the growth of black populations in poor inner-city areas, caused by poverty and segregated housing patterns due to racial discrimination.

Black mayors worked to improve the lives of African Americans. They hired more blacks for city jobs. White-controlled governments in the past had rarely hired blacks for such jobs. The mayors curbed racist treatment of blacks by local police and provided blacks with better access to housing, social services, and schools. Just as important, black residents had new hope for the future. When Bradley ran unsuccessfully for Los Angeles mayor in 1969, he explained one reason why he wanted the job: "I want to provide a sense of hope for our young people. I want [young blacks] to be able to look at city hall and know that the system can work. I want them to know that change is possible. I want them to know that in city hall sits a man with whom they can identify, that if he made it, anybody can make it."[41]

Black mayors also helped whites. They did that because it was the right thing to do and because they often needed a lot of white votes to be reelected.

Winning White Approval

Many blacks, including Bradley, have been elected mayors of cities with few black residents; blacks made up only 15 percent of the Los Angeles population when he became mayor. Other mayors elected in such cities include Norman Rice in Seattle in 1989; Wellington E. Webb in Denver in 1991; and James C. Hayes in Fairbanks, Alaska, in 1994. Hayes was born in Sacramento, California, but moved to Fairbanks when he was eight years old. He has said that he grew to love Fairbanks because residents did not care what color his skin was: "In Fairbanks, people tend to accept you as you are. They just want to hear your platform and hear what you believe in, and then see you go out and work really hard."[42] He did work hard and was reelected even though blacks accounted for only 12 percent of the city's population.

Webb was Denver mayor from 1991 to 2003. He also knew that the key to being reelected in white-majority cities was to do a good job. "Previously," Webb once said, "[blacks] were not given the chance to run, but we have shown that whether a city is in a predominantly black or white area, we can do a good job."[43] During his tenure Webb received praise for improving the city's economy by fostering commercial and residential redevelopment and reclaiming park land for citizens to enjoy along the South Platte River.

Ron Kirk was elected Dallas mayor on May 6, 1995, because he convinced white voters he could help the city improve economically as well as bring more racial harmony to a city that

Black Women Mayors

Shirley Franklin was sworn in as Atlanta mayor on January 7, 2002, to become the first female African American to head a major southern city. The first black woman elected mayor was Doris A. Davis in Compton, California, in 1973. Other women elected mayor include Sharon Pratt Kelly (Washington, D.C., 1991); Sharon Sayles Belton (Minneapolis, 1994); LaMetta Wynn (Clinton, Iowa, 1996); and Yvonne Johnson (Greensboro, North Carolina, 2007). In her inaugural address, Franklin said she was proud Atlanta voters chose her:

> It is an honor because I stand on the shoulders of all of the great leaders that this city has produced. But it is also an honor because I proudly represent all of the women who have toiled in the fields, worked in the kitchens, fought for our rights and challenged our society to ensure a better life for all of our families. This is the first time that a woman has been sworn in to serve as mayor of Atlanta. But Atlanta has always been a bold innovative city. [We] stand on the brink of a whole new era of leadership, and I am proud to lead the way.

Shirley Franklin, "Atlanta Mayoral Inauguration, January 7, 2002," City of Atlanta Online. www.atlantaga.gov/mayor/speech_inauguration.aspx.

Black women had to fight even harder to achieve political rights. Shirley Franklin succeeded in becoming mayor of Atlanta in 2002.

was 30 percent black and 21 percent Hispanic. "It doesn't matter whether your ancestors came over on the Mayflower or a slave ship. We're all in the same boat now,"[44] Kirk said in his victory speech. In two terms Kirk helped create the Trinity River Project, a $246 million plan for parks and highways in the Trinity River flood plain, and pushed construction of the American Airlines Center that opened in 2002. Both projects were considered economically beneficial for his community.

The office of mayor, however, is not the only local position in which African Americans have helped govern their communities.

The Symbolic Importance of Black Officials

Political scientists David R. Colburn and Jeffrey S. Adler believe that the election of so many black mayors has had a positive effect on the psychological outlook average blacks have for their own lives:

> Perhaps the most important aspect of African-American political ascension is the most difficult to measure. Without question, the rise of these mayors marked a fundamental symbolic turning point for African Americans. The success of [Carl B.] Stokes and [Richard G.] Hatcher, and their counterparts in other cities, gave minority city dwellers greater access to city hall. The process also contributed to the political engagement of African-Americans; according to political scientists, the success of African-American candidates changed the attitudes of African-American residents, encouraging greater interest in and knowledge of municipal affairs. Similarly, race itself no longer infuses every mayoral campaign involving an African-American candidate. Although racially charged euphemisms, such as "crack head" and "welfare queen," continue to infect campaign rhetoric, overt racism has faded considerably since 1967.

David R. Colburn and Jeffrey S. Adler, eds., *African-American Mayors: Race, Politics, and the American City*. Champaign: University of Illinois Press, 2001, p. 15.

Many Other Local Officials

As black urban populations continued to grow, they elected more black officials, and those officials gained more power. Blacks elected to city councils and county boards from Atlanta, Georgia, to San Francisco, California, initiated programs, passed laws, and wielded political power to help other blacks. In 1956 Velvalea "Vel" Phillips became the first woman and first black elected to the city council in Milwaukee, Wisconsin. During the 1960s Phillips fought to end housing discrimination that kept blacks from renting or buying homes outside the run-down inner-city area. After the council kept rejecting legislation she introduced to end such discrimination, she joined nightly protest marches and was even arrested. In 1968 the council finally approved the Fair Housing Law Phillips had first proposed six years earlier.

Many blacks fought to desegregate schools by winning election to school boards across the nation. Rachel Bassette Noel in 1965 was the first African American elected to the Denver Public Schools Board of Education as well as the first black woman elected to any public office in Colorado. On April 25, 1968, she introduced the "Noel Resolution," which sought to ensure equal educational opportunity for all children by integrating Denver schools. Even though Noel received many threatening phone calls from racist whites who opposed doing that, the board passed the resolution in February 1970. In a 2007 interview, Noel said: "I ran for the board of education so [it] would have a black voice and integrate the schools. I found there were other people [who] carried the ideas of equality, and you could be judged on your merits and not on the color of your skin."[45]

The Importance of Black Local Officials

Black local officials have helped millions of African Americans have a better life. In 2001 *Black Enterprise*, a business magazine for African Americans, surveyed its readers to find out which cities were the best for blacks to live in; seven out of the top ten cities that readers selected had black mayors, including Houston, which ranked first. Earl G. Graves wrote in the article on the survey results that since he had founded *Black Enterprise* in 1970, the number of black mayors had grown from 81 to 480, including 34 cities with populations greater than 50,000.

Graves said the survey showed how important black mayors have been in improving the lives of other blacks. He also encouraged readers of his magazine to keep electing black officials: "I cannot stress enough the importance of African Americans taking an active political role on the local level, where the rubber hits the road on everything from law enforcement and access to public transportation (i.e., getting to jobs), to neighborhood renewal and education reform."[46]

Chapter Four

Blacks Govern Their States

Virginia is the home state of Thomas Jefferson, who claimed in the Declaration of Independence in 1776 that all men had been created equal. On November 8, 1989, white Virginia voters, who outnumbered blacks four to one, elected L. Douglas Wilder their governor. In his inaugural address on January 13, 1990, Wilder noted that his election was a testament to the power of the ideal Jefferson had expressed two centuries earlier: "We mark today not the victory of party or the accomplishments of an individual, but the triumph of an idea. The idea that all men are created equally."[47] Virginia, a state that had fought during the Civil War to preserve slavery, was now governed by an African American.

Wilder was the first black elected governor and the first since Pinchback briefly served in Louisiana during Reconstruction. Although there had been a century between African American governors, there was a third one only sixteen years later in 2006 when Deval Laurdine Patrick was elected in Massachusetts. David Paterson became the fourth black governor only two years later on March 17, 2008, when he was sworn in to replace New York governor Eliot Spitzer, who resigned because of a sex scandal. Paterson, who had been the state's lieutenant governor, was also the first blind governor in U.S. history.

In 1989 Douglas Wilder became Virginia's first black governor. Wilder was popular among blacks and many whites.

Black governors were still a rarity in 2007 when Patrick took office. But by then, Patrick was one of more than six hundred black state officials, continuing a history of governing states dating back to 1836 when Twilight had been elected to the Vermont General Assembly.

A Long History of Blacks in State Government

Very few black elected officials were in state government during the twentieth century's first six decades. These pioneer officials were often subjected to racism even after they were elected. In 1957 when Cecil Partee of Chicago was elected to the Illinois House, segregation made it hard for him to find a place to stay in the state capital during legislative sessions. "When I first got there," Partee said, "it was impossible for a black legislator to live in one of the hotels."[48] Partee later served in the Illinois senate and was the first black senate president.

In 1963 a breakthrough occurred when two blacks won statewide constitutional offices—Edward W. Brooke as attorney general in Massachusetts and Gerald A. Lamb as treasurer in Connecticut. Despite their twin victories, the entire nation still had no more than 40 black state officials before Congress passed the Voting Rights Acts of 1965. Once blacks were free to vote, the number of officials grew quickly; 169 by 1970, 336 by 1980, and 423 by 1990. In 2007 the nation's more than 600 black state officials included 40 elected to statewide positions, including Patrick and lieutenant governors Anthony Brown of Maryland and David A. Paterson of New York.

Political analysts believe Patrick's election was made easier by Wilder's victory in 1989. That is because Wilder had shattered a racial barrier in politics years before that some whites had thought might never be broken.

Wild About Wilder

The first elected black governor was the grandson of slaves, but his father was an insurance salesman who provided Wilder and his seven brothers and sisters with a good home. Wilder graduated in 1952 from Virginia Union University, a black college in Richmond. He then enlisted in the army and fought in the Korean conflict, where he won a medal for bravery. After getting his law degree from Howard University in 1959, Wilder opened a law practice in his hometown. Wilder became involved in politics and in 1969 was the first black elected to the Virginia senate since Reconstruction.

In his first senate speech in February 1970, Wilder asked Virginia to quit using "Carry Me Back to Old Virginia" as its state song because of offensive lyrics that referred to blacks as "darkies." The state kept the song, but Wilder became popular with fellow African Americans by backing such civil rights causes. He won white supporters by championing fiscally conservative policies to keep taxes low and working to strengthen the state's economy.

Wilder became so popular that in 1985 he was elected lieutenant governor to become the first black to hold statewide executive office in the South since Reconstruction. Wilder said he hoped his election victory would show other African Americans that they could accomplish great things despite lingering racism. "You can't give up, you can't believe that your origin, your birth status must be a detraction,"[49] he said.

Four years later Wilder was elected governor when he narrowly defeated Republican J. Marshall Coleman 896,936 votes to 890,195. The voting was so close that the state ordered a recount of ballots. Wilder won by 6,741 votes, or less than half a percent, in the tightest race for governor in the state's history.

After Wilder won, he claimed that his victory in a state with a black population of only 19 percent showed that voters did not care about race. Said Wilder: "It is not and it was not a factor in the results—because I was elected."[50] Election returns, however,

L. Douglas Wilder Earned His Success

L. Douglas Wilder became Virginia's first black lieutenant governor in 1986. An article in Richmond's *Times–Dispatch* newspaper explains how he earned his political victory:

Growing up [in Richmond, Virginia], he and his seven brothers and sisters would beg their father, insurance salesman Robert J. Wilder, to tell them again and again about how his parents, and even his older siblings, had been slaves. Today's white majority can only imagine the pathos behind those stories told on a paternal lap. But in overcoming a legacy of racial supremacy and discrimination to be elected lieutenant governor, Doug Wilder never acted as though the world owed him anything. Instead [he] went out and earned it. He has credited his mother, Beulah, who made him learn a new word each and every day, with instilling in him the drive to excel. If people want to take a message from his victory, he told one interviewer, he hopes it will be that "you can't give up, you can't believe that your origin, your birth status must be a detraction," and that "young people will see the value of staying in school, of directing their life away from the wastefulness of crime."

Richmond Times-Dispatch, "Inaugural History," January 12, 1986, p. A22.

showed that it did matter to some Virginians—in some heavily white districts, Wilder did not get as many votes as other Democratic candidates. His election was also by a very narrow margin, which meant that many people who did not support Wilder were ready to criticize whatever he did as governor.

The Wilder Era

The new governor faced a difficult challenge in Virginia because he had to immediately deal with a $2.2 billion state budget deficit. Wilder erased the deficit by freezing state hiring and making deep cuts in spending. He won praise for that accomplishment as well as for appointing a record number of minorities and women to state jobs and initiating a law to slow the sale of handguns to stem violence. Some people, however, became angry that his budget cut programs that they liked.

Wilder was also criticized for traveling extensively; one newspaper reported that he was outside of the state at least two hundred of his first six hundred days as governor. Some trips were related to Wilder's duties, such as visits to foreign countries to increase business opportunities for Virginia. However, Wilder also traveled to further his political career. Wilder believed he could use the prestige of being the first black governor to win the Democratic nomination for president. But when Wilder's candidacy flopped, he dropped out of the race in January 1992 to concentrate on governing Virginia. Wilder admitted then that "balancing the rigors of running a state government and conducting a national campaign have not been easy."[51] By that time, Wilder had angered many more Virginians who believed he hurt his state by spending so much time seeking a higher office.

In his final two years in office, Wilder had mixed success as governor, mainly because Virginia continued to struggle financially due to a national economic recession. Most people believed Wilder could not have won reelection, but in Virginia, governors are limited to one term. In his last appearance as governor in January 1994, Wilder said he hoped other blacks would be inspired by his political achievement: "I hope my election was merely the opening of the door for many opportunities for others, who, in many instances, are far more qualified than myself."[52]

Wilder's election had shown the nation that an African American was capable of being elected and governing a state. There would not be another black governor, however, until November 7, 2006, when Patrick was elected in Massachusetts.

The Third Black Governor

The nation's third black governor was born on July 31, 1956. Three years later his father abandoned the family, and he lived with his mother and sister in a two-bedroom apartment in a poor, gang-infested area on Chicago's South Side. In 1970 the fourteen-year-old received a scholarship to Milton Academy, a prep school near Boston, Massachusetts. The move changed his life as he received a superior education. He then went on to graduate from Harvard and Harvard Law School.

The public did not know much about Patrick when he entered the governor's race in January 2005. Patrick made headlines as head of the U.S. Justice Department's Civil Rights Division from 1994 to 1997, but after that he worked in virtual anonymity as a federal judge and executive for Texaco and Coca Cola Co. But Patrick quickly won support from blacks and whites. People were drawn to Patrick because of his charismatic personality—he is an inspirational speaker—and their belief that his corporate and government experience would make him a good governor.

Patrick won 56 percent of the vote to easily defeat Republican lieutenant governor Kerry Healey. On January 3, 2007, the day before he was sworn in as governor, Patrick spoke to a thousand blacks after a religious service at Boston's Jubilee Christian Church. Patrick said, "We are an enduring people, we are a lasting people, and we have been counted out for centuries, but we keep defying expectations."[53] Patrick himself was an African American who had defied expectations by winning in a predominantly white state.

In his first year as governor, Patrick created a $26.8 billion budget that increased state aid to education. He also proposed a $1.1 billion bond issue to fund affordable housing and began studying the feasibility of giving every resident a free community college education. Patrick also continued speaking out for the rights of minorities. On Martin Luther King Jr. Day on January 15, 2007, he said, "The notion of equality is never even mentioned in public

Deval Patrick is sworn in as Massachusetts's first black governor in January 2007.

discourse today. Race relations is the only major social ill we seem seriously to be considering curing by denial."[54] Patrick also told people to respect the rights of Latinos, Asians, and gay people.

Patrick was doing what other black officials had always done—working to erase the injustices that made life hard for many African Americans.

Black State Legislators

In 1989 Wisconsin state representative Polly Williams drafted a bill to allow poor parents, black or white, to choose which

Justice and Fair Play

On March 29, 1921, two African American state legislators urged the Pennsylvania General Assembly to [pass] an equal rights bill [to end racial discrimination]. John C. Asbury, a Republican representative from Philadelphia, spoke of his interracial upbringing in Washington County: "As a boy, I played, studied, and fought with boys of other races. I never received anything from those boys but justice and fair play. In the belief that Pennsylvania men are just Pennsylvania boys grown older, I come to you asking for that same justice and fair play." Republican Andrew Stevens Jr. of Philadelphia reminded his colleagues that it was Easter, a time to remember that Christ died so "that the sins of men might be redeemed—not white men, brown men or even yellow men or black men, but all men." Stevens argued that if all men have equal access to salvation, then all men are entitled to equal rights under the law. By this bill, Stevens said, blacks "demand full citizenship in Pennsylvania and these United States of America." [The bill was defeated.]

Eric Ledell Smith, "'Asking for Justice and Fair Play': African American State Legislators and Civil Rights in Early Twentieth-Century Pennsylvania." *Pennsylvania History*, April 1996, pp. 2–3.

schools their children attended. Williams, who had represented a black district in Milwaukee since 1980, proposed a voucher program to give low-income families state funds so they could enroll their children in private schools. Williams believed private schools provided a better education than public schools; she wanted poor families to have the choice of sending their children to such schools even though they could not afford them. "I represent poor people," Williams said. "And I felt that choice was a valuable tool of empowerment for poor people. It was that simple."[55]

Williams acted because she knew that getting a good education was the best way for young people from poor families to improve their lives. The legislature approved the program, but Williams's "simple" idea quickly spread far beyond her home state.

The nation's first school choice program ignited a nationwide movement to allow families more power in choosing schools for their children.

Although few black state legislators have had such a powerful impact nationally, several have wielded extreme political power in their own states. Willie L. Brown Jr. represented San Francisco in the California State Assembly for three decades, and from 1980 to 1995 he was assembly Speaker. As Speaker, Brown was able to control the legislation that the eighty-member assembly created. In the process, Brown became one of the most influential political figures the state had ever known. Another powerful state legislator was Charles Walker, who in 1996 became majority leader in the Georgia senate.

By 2007 a total of 624 blacks served in state legislatures, and even states with small black populations had several black lawmakers. In 2002, for example, seven of Nevada's sixty-three legislators—11 percent—were black, even though only 6.8 percent of Nevada residents were African American. Woodrow Wilson became Nevada's first black legislator when he was elected to the assembly in 1966, and Joe Neal became Nevada's first black state senator six years later. In 2002 Neal, still a state senator, explained why Nevada voters were electing so many blacks:

"There has been a change. If you meet the voters and explain the issues to them and they are affected by those issues, then they will vote for you. You just have to get out and let people know who you are. People seem to have gained a liking to black elected officials. They aren't afraid to vote for them."[56]

Some blacks, however, have not been welcomed by white lawmakers when they were elected. When Mervyn Dymally entered the California State Assembly in 1962, there were only three other black legislators. He said white legislators ignored them and sometimes offended them with racial slurs: "I went to a luncheon one day, and as I got up to leave for another appointment, a [Democratic state legislator] used the N-word. (Afterward), they all came up to apologize to me."[57] By 1967, however, there were six blacks in the California legislature, and whites had to start respecting African Americans more because their political power was growing.

Black influence in California government increased in 1974 when Dymally was elected lieutenant governor, the first African

American to hold a California statewide office. Dymally, however, was one of many blacks to hold statewide office across the nation.

Black State Elected Officials

In 1960 Otis M. Smith was elected Michigan's auditor general to become the first black to win a statewide election since Reconstruction. In 1963 two blacks won statewide office—Lamb as treasurer in Connecticut and Brooke as attorney general in Massachusetts—and dozens of blacks have held such positions since then. Many black state officials began as state legislators, but not all of them. In 1978 Phillips, the first black member of the Milwaukee Common Council and Wisconsin's first black judge, was elected Wisconsin's secretary of state. She was Wisconsin's first black statewide constitutional official.

When Patrick was elected in 2006, Anthony Brown was elected lieutenant governor of Maryland, and five other blacks were re-elected to statewide offices they already held—New York lieutenant governor Paterson, Georgia attorney general Thurbert Baker, Illinois secretary of state Jesse White, Connecticut treasurer Denise Nappier, and Georgia commissioner of labor Michael Thurmond.

For Anthony Brown, being lieutenant governor was a big change from being a member of the Maryland House of Delegates. Brown said in an interview about his new job, "The days are long, they're busy, they're full of all sorts of activities."[58] Brown's major concerns his first year were working to strengthen community colleges, economic development, health care, and veterans' affairs. He even represented the state on a trade mission to China.

Nappier was already accustomed to the rigors of her job because she had been Connecticut treasurer since 1999. One of the causes Nappier has adopted is affordable housing. In November 2007 in Stamford, Connecticut, Nappier said, "We should all be shocked and outraged that it takes an hourly housing wage of $30.62 to afford a typical two-bedroom apartment in the Stamford-Norwalk area."[59] Nappier said she and other state officials are working to provide more low-cost housing throughout Connecticut.

Being elected a state official gives blacks an opportunity to help other blacks. Sometimes their election is also an opportunity for them to heal old racial wounds.

The Many "Firsts" of Vel Phillips

Few black public officials have recorded more firsts than Velvalea "Vel" Phillips, who in 1978 was elected secretary of state to become the first woman and first African American to win a statewide constitutional office in Wisconsin. When Governor Jim Doyle declared "Vel Phillips Day" in Wisconsin on April 7, 2006, he noted her many accomplishments:

> Vel Phillips has built a career full of "firsts" as both a woman and an African American in Wisconsin. Vel Phillips [was] the first African American woman to graduate from the University of Wisconsin–Madison Law School in 1951. As an Alderwoman in Milwaukee [in 1956 she was the first black and woman elected to the City Council], she worked to pass the city's first open-housing ordinance in 1968. She was appointed the first woman judge in Milwaukee and the first African American judge in Wisconsin in 1971. [She] has, and continues to, work tirelessly to help establish equality and opportunity for people of color through social justice, education, and employment and equal housing opportunities.

> James Doyle, "A Proclamation: Governor Doyle Proclaims Today 'Vel Phillips Day' in the State of Wisconsin." Office of the Governor, April 7, 2007. www.wisgov.state.wi.us/journal_media_detail.asp?locid=19&prid=1894.

Wisconsin Common Council president Marvin Pratt takes the oath of office as acting mayor from Secretary of State Vel Phillips.

Revenge for Her Father

Verda Freeman Welcome was teaching in Baltimore schools in the 1950s when she became involved in the fight to integrate that city's public facilities. As part of that battle, Welcome in 1958 ran for and won a seat in the Maryland House of Delegates, and four years later she was elected to the state senate. Welcome had become committed to the crusade for black rights as a young woman in North Carolina when she saw her father abused by whites when he tried to vote. Welcome vowed then that "one day I am going to vote and pay back the insult to my father."[60] Welcome not only voted but was elected so she could write laws for her adopted state.

Chapter Five

Blacks Write Laws for the Entire Nation

The Democratic Party in the 2006 fall election captured a majority of seats in the U.S. House of Representatives. That gave the Democrats the right to name chairpersons of every House committee, including the Ways and Means Committee, which is the most powerful because it originates every spending bill. Representative Charles Rangel of New York, who had been a congressman for more than three decades, was named chairman of that key committee. The position gave Rangel more political power than any African American congressman had ever had. Rangel claimed the assignment did not affect his life except to make him work harder but admitted that many blacks he met were excited about his new position. In November 2007 he said: "I was in South Carolina recently, and a guy brought me his grandson and said he was so excited to have the kid shake the hand of the chairman of the powerful Ways and Means Committee. And the kid grabbed my hand and asked, 'What was the Ways and Means Committee?' And the grandfather said, 'I don't know, but it's awesome.'"[61]

Senator Charles Rangel was named chairman of the House Ways and Means Committee in 2006.

Several other blacks in 2007 were named chairpersons of key committees, including John Conyers of Michigan to the Judiciary Committee and Bennie Thompson of Mississippi to the Committee on Homeland Security. The important assignments showed how much black political strength had grown in Congress since the early twentieth century.

From One to Many

On November 6, 1928, De Priest of Illinois became the first black elected from a northern state and the first black congressman since North Carolina's George Henry White in 1901. De Priest was also the last African American Republican congressman until Gary Franks of Connecticut in 1990. During the 1920s almost all black voters switched their allegiance to the Democratic Party because President Franklin D. Roosevelt's social welfare policies helped them and because the Democratic Party began courting them.

Congress had never had more than one black member until Adam Clayton Powell of New York was elected in 1945 to join William L. Dawson of Illinois. The handful of African American congressmen in the twentieth century's first six decades discovered that even their powerful positions could not protect them from discrimination. In 1934 De Priest's son was refused service at the restaurant Congress operates for its members and visitors. De Priest fought to allow all blacks to eat there, claiming that "if we allow segregation and the denial of constitutional rights under the dome of the capitol, where in God's name will we [blacks] get them?"[62] A congressional committee investigated the incident but refused to overturn the racist policy.

Powell was angered when he arrived because the congressional barbershop refused to cut his hair. But in 1946 Powell made his legislative mark in Congress when he introduced the "Powell Amendment" to a spending bill. The measure forced companies with federal contracts to hire black workers. Powell added it to bills for the next two decades because he believed African Americans should benefit from jobs created by federal programs they helped fund with their taxes. Said Powell: "The black masses must demand and refuse to accept nothing less than the proportionate share of political jobs and appointments which are equal to their proportion in the electorate."[63]

There were few black congressmen until the 1960s, but their numbers grew steadily after that. African Americans significantly increased their representation in Congress in 1992 when thirteen new members were elected to raise their total to thirty-eight. Representative Edolphus Towns of New York claimed that the increase "is clear evidence of the enhanced power and political influence of African-Americans."[64] One of the new members of Congress in 1992 was Carol Moseley Braun of Illinois, the first black woman elected to the U.S. Senate. Her election, however, came twenty-six years after Brooke had become the twentieth century's first African American senator.

The First Black Elected U.S. Senator

Edward W. Brooke claims race was not an issue in his 1966 election as a U.S. senator:

Insofar as race was an issue, it was largely unspoken. Because our state's African American population was so small, perhaps 2 percent of the voters, I shook mostly white hands, looked into mostly white faces, and with very few exceptions, saw no anger in their eyes. [No citizen] asked me about the burden of being an African American running for the Senate, but reporters must have asked me in a thousand ways if race would hurt my chances. [I] told the press that I was proud of my heritage but that being an African American had not hurt me in my previous campaigns, so I did not see why it should hurt me now. That, I thought, was the real story—not that my race would hurt me but that it would not. The endless questions about my race sometimes annoyed me, but I could not complain. The media gave us the kind of coverage that we could never have bought.

Edward W. Brooke, *Bridging the Divide: My Life*. New Brunswick, NJ: Rutgers University Press, 2007, pp. 136–37.

The Senator from Massachusetts

The first black senator since Reconstruction was born on October 26, 1919, in Washington, D.C. Brooke, whose father was a lawyer for the federal Veterans Administration, once admitted that racism did not greatly mar his childhood: "I know the dreadful discrimination and bigotry which many American Negroes have suffered, but honestly I cannot claim that this had any shattering effect on me."[65] After graduating from Howard University in 1941, Brooke fought in World War II with a segregated black unit in the U.S. Army. After the war Brooke went to Boston University Law School, settled in Massachusetts, and entered politics. Brooke lost his first three campaigns—for the state legislature in 1950 and 1952 and secretary of state in 1960—before winning the 1962 election for attorney general.

In four years as attorney general, Brooke convicted several Republican lawmakers on conflict of interest charges even though he was a Republican. His political impartiality and his fine work on other issues impressed Massachusetts voters. On November 8, 1966, they elected him senator of a state in which blacks made up only 2 percent of the population. Brooke was the first black elected to the Senate by popular vote; Reconstruction senators Revels and Bruce were elected by the Mississippi legislature.

In the Senate, Brooke continued to vote his conscience rather than his party affiliation. He voted against three people Republican president Richard Nixon nominated for the U.S. Supreme Court because he considered them unfit candidates. He also criticized Nixon for failing to keep his 1968 presidential campaign promise to end the Vietnam War quickly. "I was proud to be a

Edward Brooke became a senator for Massachusetts in 1966. He claims that prejudice did not really affect him.

Republican," Brooke once said, "but my ultimate loyalty was to certain goals and ideals, not to party."[66]

Brooke served two terms before being defeated in 1978. It would be fourteen more years before Braun was elected to become the first black woman senator.

Black Women in Congress

When Braun was elected in 1992, she was one of just six black women in Congress. Only four years later, the female black contingent more than doubled as a dozen women were elected to the House to join Braun, whose six-year term as a senator continued. Newcomer Carolyn Cheeks Kilpatrick of Detroit explained why so many black women were elected:

> I think women innately come from God with certain skills and characteristics that make it possible for them to build bridges and work [with other people] in a way to get things done. I think you have African-American females who have excelled as the 13 of us have [and] we bring such traits as intelligence, hard work, dedication and sensitivity to the people we represent.[67]

The new congresswomen all owed part of their success to the first black woman elected to Congress—Shirley Chisholm. Born in Brooklyn, New York, on November 30, 1924, the graduate of Columbia University was elected to the New York state legislature in 1964 and four years later defeated civil rights leader James Farmer for a seat in Congress. After her victory, Chisholm had declared, "Just wait, there may be some fireworks."[68] She created them in fourteen years in office by fighting hard to help poor people, both black and white. Chisholm backed spending increases for education, health care, and other social services. She also opposed the Vietnam War and the military draft, which she claimed resulted in a disproportionate number of blacks being sent to fight in Vietnam.

In 1972 Chisholm, a Democrat, made history again as the first black woman to campaign for a major party's presidential nomination. Even though she knew she had no chance of winning, Chisholm ran because she wanted to show that a black woman had the right to seek the nation's highest office. That was part of

Shirley Chisholm Stands Up for Women

Shirley Chisholm in 1968 became the first black woman elected to Congress. In her book *Unbought and Unbossed*, Chisholm explained that she had to overcome "the double drawbacks" of sexism against women and racism against blacks to accomplish that:

> Why are women herded into jobs as secretaries, librarians, and teachers and discouraged from being managers, lawyers, doctors, and members of Congress? Because it is assumed that they are different from men. Today's new militant campaigners for women's rights have made the point that for a long time society discriminated against blacks on the same basis: they were different and inferior. The cheerful old darky on the plantation and the happy little homemaker are equally stereotypes drawn by prejudice. White America is beginning to be able to admit that it carries racial prejudice in its heart, and that understanding marks the beginning of the end of racism. But prejudice against women is still acceptable because it is invisible. Few men can be persuaded to believe that it exists. Many women, even, are the same way.

Shirley Chisholm, *Unbought and Unbossed.* Boston: Houghton Mifflin, 1970, pp. 163–64.

During her political career, Shirley Chisholm fought for America's poor and against the military draft.

the legacy Chisholm once said she wanted to leave: "I do not want to be remembered as the first black woman elected to Congress. I do not even want to be remembered as the first to run for president. I want to be remembered as a woman who fought for change in the twentieth century. That is what I want."[69]

Chisholm, who died on January 1, 2005, successfully shattered several political barriers for black women. Braun also made history for women and blacks when she was elected.

A Black Woman Senator

Braun's victory in an election for a U.S. Senate seat was the biggest political surprise of 1992. The University of Chicago Law School graduate held the unimportant position of Cook County recorder of deeds when she challenged Senator Alan Dixon. Even though Braun had been a state legislator for a decade before that, she seemed mismatched against an incumbent senator. Even she admitted after her election that she had been an unlikely candidate: "I was female, working class and black. I joked it was a triple-dose of diversity."[70]

Dixon crippled his chance to win when he voted to confirm Clarence Thomas as a U.S. Supreme Court justice. The vote alienated many women who disliked Thomas because he had been accused of sexually harassing Anita Hill, a coworker. And even though Thomas was African American, many blacks scorned him because he was a conservative who opposed policies they favored, such as affirmative action. The negative response to the vote helped Braun defeat Dixon.

Although Braun was elected with great fanfare, her image became tarnished before she even took office. She was criticized for visiting South Africa after the election with Kgosie Matthews, her boyfriend and campaign manager, instead of preparing for her new job. Allegations also surfaced that Matthews had misused campaign funds. However, Braun generally performed ably as a senator. A highlight of her one term came in July 1993 when she persuaded the Senate to deny the United Daughters of the Confederacy the right to continue using an insignia that included the Confederate flag. In an impassioned speech, Braun explained that many people considered the flag a racist symbol: "This vote is about race. It is about racial symbols, the racial past, and the single most painful episode in American history [the Civil War]. It is absolutely unacceptable to me and to millions of Americans, black or white, that we would put the imprimatur of the United States Senate on a symbol of this kind of idea."[71]

Braun made her biggest blunder in 1996 when she visited Nigeria to meet General Sani Abacha, a dictator who had executed political opponents. She went because Matthews was now working for a lobbying firm that supported Abacha. That issue and other problems Braun had as a senator helped Republican Peter Fitzgerald defeat her in 1998.

Fitzgerald would also be a one-term senator as he would lose his reelection campaign in 2004 to another African American—Barack Hussein Obama.

Another Black Senator

The fifth African American senator in U.S. history was born on August 4, 1961, in Honolulu, Hawaii, to Barack Obama Sr., a native of Kenya, Africa, and Ann Dunham, who is white. Obama graduated from Harvard Law School in 1991 and moved to Chicago,

Barack Obama campaigns for president in 2007. Obama's bid for the presidency was groundbreaking in many ways.

where he practiced law and became involved in politics. In 1996 Obama was elected to the Illinois senate, where he won praise for helping draft laws on health care and welfare and curbing race-motivated arrests by police. Obama was a candidate for the U.S. Senate when he gave the keynote speech on July 27, 2004, at the Democratic National Convention. The acclaim Obama got from his speech helped him defeat Fitzgerald.

Obama became a fierce Senate opponent of the Iraq War. He also helped draft legislation on immigration reform, security for the U.S. border, and election fraud. His accomplishments and his engaging personality made Obama a rising star in the Democratic Party. Many people liked Obama because he had a sense of humor about himself. He often joked about how confused people are that he has a Muslim name—he is a Christian—and speaks without a black accent:

"When I first ran for state Senate [people] would call me 'Yo Mama.' And I'd have to explain, 'No, it's O-bama'—that my father was from Kenya, from Africa, which is where I got the name . . . and that my mother was from Kansas, which is why I talk the way I do."[72]

The prominence Obama gained in the Senate led him on February 10, 2007, to announce his candidacy for president. Political analysts claimed he was the first black to have a legitimate chance to win that office.

A New Level of Political Power

Obama's candidacy was symbolic of the new political power blacks wielded in Congress after a record forty African Americans were elected to Congress in November 2006. It was a strength made up not only of numbers but the important committee assignments blacks now held. When majority parties choose committee chairpersons, they select the committee member who has served the most years in Congress. Because some committee members have twenty or even thirty years of seniority, it took decades for blacks to win the right to gain those important positions. Rangel said it was important that blacks had finally won such powerful positions because "now we are at the table to give our views."[73] And in 2007 they began flexing their newly won political muscle to affect legislation and government policy.

African American Presidential Candidates

When Senator Barack Obama in 2007 announced he was running for president, the Illinois Democrat was one of a long line of African Americans who have been candidates for the nation's highest office. The first black nominated to run for vice president was Frederick Douglass, a former slave who was one of the nineteenth century's most powerful leaders in the fight for black rights. The Equal Rights Party in 1872 chose him as the running mate for Victoria Woodhull, the first female to run for president. Douglass never campaigned because the party chose him without his consent. Senator Blanche Kelso Bruce of Mississippi in 1880 received eight votes for vice president at the Republican Party convention. James W. Ford in 1932 was the first African American on a presidential ticket in the twentieth century; he was the Communist Party USA vice presidential candidate. U.S. representative Shirley Chisholm in 1972 was the first black woman to run for president. Other Democratic candidates have been civil rights leader Jesse Jackson in 1984 and 1988, Alan Keyes in 1996 and in 2000, and black activist Al Sharpton and former U.S. senator Carol Moseley Braun in 2004.

On October 25 Rangel released details of a $1.3 trillion tax reform proposal. The bill provides tax relief for most people while raising taxes for those earning several hundred thousand dollars a year. Because overhauling the tax system is one of the most significant ways in which Congress affects the nation, it showed how much power one black congressman now had. Rangel himself boasted about what his bill could accomplish: "Ninety million people are going to get a tax cut. It has been more than 21 years since Congress and the administration rolled up their sleeves to discuss tax reform, and during that time the tax code has become a jumbled mess of outdated and inequitable provisions that cry out for simplification."[74]

Conyers was also dealing with bills that directly affected the lives of citizens. The Homeland Security Committee he chaired dealt with issues concerning the nation's war on terrorism from fighting in Iraq to how to protect Americans from terrorist attacks. One of the most controversial issues in 2007 was whether the Central Intelligence Agency (CIA) had tortured prisoners during the Iraq War. When the CIA was accused of destroying videotapes that showed such torture to conceal the behavior from Congress, Conyers and others called for a special investigation to find out what happened. Conyers in January 2008 claimed, "The potential obstruction of justice alleged in the controversy over the CIA's detainee torture tape destruction is a serious matter."[75] Conyers's criticism was important because of the committee he headed.

"We, the People"

The power that African Americans wield in Congress today stands in stark contrast to the long periods in U.S. history during which they had no say in governing their nation. On July 25, 1974, Representative Barbara Jordan of Texas commented in a speech to the House Judiciary Committee on how black political power was already growing. Jordan said:

> [The U.S. Constitution begins] "We, the people." It's a very eloquent beginning. But when that document was completed on the seventeenth of September in 1787, I was not included in that "We, the people." I felt somehow for many years that George Washington and Alexander Hamilton just left me out by mistake. But through the process of amendment, interpretation, and court decision, I have finally been included in "We, the people."[76]

Chapter Six

Black Appointed Officials Also Govern

On January 26, 2005, Condoleezza Rice was sworn in as the nation's sixty-sixth secretary of state. Rice was the first black woman to hold that position but not the first African American—that honor belonged to her predecessor, Colin Powell. Rice that day fulfilled a vow she made when she visited Washington, D.C., with her parents. As Condoleezza was walking past the White House, she told her father "Daddy, I'm barred out of there now because of the color of my skin. But one day, I'll be in that house."[77] In 1964 working in the White House seemed an impossible dream for a ten-year-old black girl. Rice grew up in Birmingham, Alabama, and had already experienced the pain of being called racist names and barred from white restaurants.

But civil rights victories in the 1960s made that dream possible, and Rice made it a reality by becoming an expert on international politics. Rice wielded as much power as any African American official ever did, even though she had not been elected. She was one of thousands of officials at all levels of government throughout the United States who were appointed to

Two powerful black political leaders confer. Former U.S. secretary of state Colin Powell speaks with his successor, Condoleezza Rice.

their positions by elected officials or governmental bodies. The black appointed officials included police and fire chiefs, school superintendents, and state and federal judges. Few blacks were ever appointed to such positions until the Voting Rights Act of 1965. But the number of such black officeholders and the prestige of their positions have both increased since then because of the growth of black voting power.

The most symbolically important appointment of a black official occurred on June 13, 1967, when President Lyndon B. Johnson nominated Thurgood Marshall to the U.S. Supreme Court. The high court for nearly a century after Reconstruction had allowed states to illegally deny blacks their civil rights, and

Marshall himself had been a victim of that failure of the U.S. justice system.

The First Black Justice

In 1930 the University of Maryland Law School refused to admit Marshall because he was black. Marshall was born July 2, 1908, in Baltimore, Maryland, and he had been subjected to such racist treatment his entire life while living in the South. But that particular snub made him so angry that he decided to dedicate his life to fighting for black equality: "They wouldn't let me go to the law school because I was a Negro [so] when I got out and passed the bar [to become a lawyer], I proceeded to make them pay for it. I enjoyed it to no end."[78]

After graduating from Howard University Law School, Marshall became a civil rights lawyer for the National Association

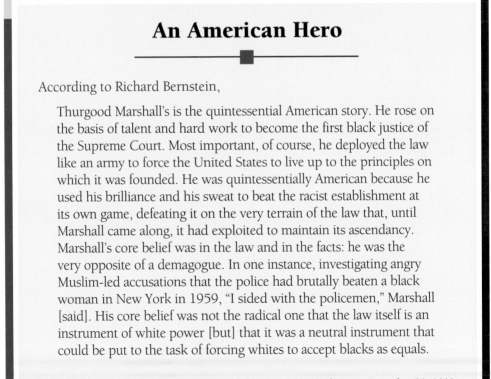

An American Hero

According to Richard Bernstein,

> Thurgood Marshall's is the quintessential American story. He rose on the basis of talent and hard work to become the first black justice of the Supreme Court. Most important, of course, he deployed the law like an army to force the United States to live up to the principles on which it was founded. He was quintessentially American because he used his brilliance and his sweat to beat the racist establishment at its own game, defeating it on the very terrain of the law that, until Marshall came along, it had exploited to maintain its ascendancy. Marshall's core belief was in the law and in the facts: he was the very opposite of a demagogue. In one instance, investigating angry Muslim-led accusations that the police had brutally beaten a black woman in New York in 1959, "I sided with the policemen," Marshall [said]. His core belief was not the radical one that the law itself is an instrument of white power [but] that it was a neutral instrument that could be put to the task of forcing whites to accept blacks as equals.

Richard Bernstein, "A Civil Rights Hero Inside the Law," *New York Times*, December 30, 1998, p. E12.

for the Advancement of Colored People (NAACP). Marshall won twenty of the thirty-two cases he argued before the Supreme Court. His biggest victory was in *Brown v. Board of Education of Topeka*. Marshall argued that the segregated school system in Topeka, Kansas, was illegal because black schools were inferior to those for whites. In a unanimous 9–0 decision on May 17, 1954, the Court ruled that school segregation was illegal. Marshall was

Supreme Court associate justice Thurgood Marshall was instrumental in the *Brown v. Board of Education of Topeka* decision.

overjoyed with the verdict—"I was so happy, I was numb,"[79] he said—because Supreme Court decisions affect the entire nation. The ruling ended segregated school systems and made Marshall nationally known.

In 1961 President John F. Kennedy appointed Marshall to the U.S. Court of Appeals and in 1965 Johnson named him solicitor general, the official who represents the nation before the Supreme Court. Marshall won fourteen of the nineteen cases he argued for the government, more than any other solicitor general. When Johnson named Marshall to the high court, southern senators tried but failed to block his nomination. The Senate confirmed Marshall on August 30, 1967, and he served with distinction for twenty-four years. When he retired, a reporter asked Marshall what he wanted historians to say about him. Marshall answered "He did the best he could with what he had."[80]

President George H.W. Bush on July 2, 1991, nominated Clarence Thomas to replace Marshall. When Thomas was confirmed on October 19, 1991, the nation's second black justice joined a growing number of black federal judges.

An Increase in Black Judges

There were no black federal judges until 1937 when William H. Hastie was appointed to the U.S. District Court of the Virgin Islands, a U.S. territory. The first black federal judge in the continental United States was James B. Parsons, who on August 9, 1961, became a U.S. district judge in Illinois. Kennedy telephoned him early one morning to tell him of his appointment, but Parsons was so angry someone woke him up that he began berating the caller. "When I paused," Parsons said years later, "this voice came on the phone and said, 'But judge, this is President Kennedy.'"[81] Parsons immediately calmed down and heard the historic news. There were nearly seventy black federal judges when Parsons retired in 1992. Their numbers swelled under President Bill Clinton, who from 1992 to 2000 appointed sixty-two judges, which was just two fewer than the five preceding presidents combined had named.

There were few black judges at any level when Parsons was chosen. In 1852 Robert Morris became the nation's first black judge when he was appointed to magistrate's court in Boston. African American judges remained a rarity for more than a century

The Courage of One Black Official

William H. Hastie in 1937 became the nation's first black federal judge when he was appointed to the U.S. District Court of the Virgin Islands. During World War II Hastie also served as a civilian aide to the War Department. He was angered at the racist treatment of black soldiers, who were segregated into black units and treated in a racist manner by other soldiers. When army officers and federal officials refused to stop the racist treatment, Hastie quit. Hastie claimed that:

> The traditional mores of the South have been widely accepted and adopted by the Army as the basis of policy and practice affecting the Negro soldiers. In tactical organization, in physical location, in human contacts, the Negro soldier is separated from the White soldier as completely as possible. Insistence upon an inflexible policy of separating White and Black soldiers is probably the most dramatic evidence of hypocrisy [in the nation's stated goal of fighting in World War II] for the preservation of democracy. [Racism] will not be changed overnight. The disturbing thing is that there is no apparent disposition to make a beginning [to end it].

Lerone Bennett Jr., "Chronicles of Black Courage," *Ebony*, September 1994, p. 72.

Federal judge William Hastie, pictured in Washington, D.C., in 1949.

after that. However, in 1939 New York mayor Fiorello LaGuardia named Jane Bolin to the city's family court, making her the nation's first black woman judge.

It took even longer for a black to sit on a state supreme court, which is powerful because it reviews decisions of lower state courts. In 1955 Governor W. Averell Harriman named Harold A. Stevens to the New York State supreme court and in 1972 Robert Nelson Cornelius Nix Jr., of Pennsylvania became the first black chief justice of a state supreme court. Leah Ward Sears of Georgia in 2005 became the first black female to head a state supreme court. Ward, who began preparing for a career in law at age seven, loved being a judge: "This is what I really always wanted to do, hear the big issues of the day."[82]

It was a long time before blacks could make those important decisions. It also took them many years to become top presidential advisers and cabinet members.

Black Advisers and Cabinet Members

Presidents have the power to appoint people to head federal agencies like the State Department and Defense Department. These important federal officials also become key advisers to the president and collectively are known as the president's cabinet. The first black cabinet member was Robert Weaver. Johnson on January 18, 1966, named Weaver secretary of the Department of Housing and Urban Development (HUD). It was not the first time, however, that Weaver had been a presidential adviser. In the 1930s President Franklin D. Roosevelt had begun consulting with African Americans on issues that affected them because he wanted the support of the growing number of black voters. Weaver and the other African American advisers became known as his "black cabinet."

Johnson knew that Weaver had earned the honor of being the first African American cabinet member through decades of fighting for equality for blacks, including a stint as chairman of the National Association for the Advancement of Colored People. Johnson also knew Weaver had the perfect personality to withstand scrutiny by whites, some of them racist, who would watch closely to see how a black would perform in such an important position. Weaver was famous for the calm yet confident manner in which he had always battled racism. He once described that as "Fight hard and legally and don't blow your top."[83]

Although President Jimmy Carter in 1977 made Patricia Roberts Harris the first black female cabinet member when he named her to head HUD, there were few black cabinet members after that until Clinton was elected in 1992. In two terms, Clinton appointed seven blacks to his cabinet, including commerce secretary Ron Brown and Alexis Herman, the first female labor secretary. Herman, like Weaver, brought to her cabinet post lessons that had been learned in the civil rights battle. The lessons Herman learned, however, had been handed down to her by her father, Alex Herman, who had risked his life to integrate Alabama's Democratic Party. In May 1997 when Herman was sworn in as labor secretary by vice president Al Gore, she said, "He taught me that you have to face adversity. He taught me to stand by my principles. He also taught me how to work within the system for change."[84]

Clinton also named Joycelyn Elders the first black U.S. surgeon general and appointed nine African Americans presidential assistants. When Clinton left office in January 2001, presidential assistant Ben Johnson boasted: "We were the most diverse White House in the history of the country—and the most successful. When you look at this White House compared to others, it is phenomenal. He has clearly done more for Black Americans than any other president in history."[85]

Clinton did so much for blacks that he once jokingly referred to himself as the nation's first "black president." However, two people appointed by President George W. Bush—Powell and Rice—would become the most famous black cabinet members in U.S. history.

Powell, Rice, and the Iraq War

On October 1, 1989, Powell capped a distinguished career in the U.S. Army by being named the first black chairman of the Joint Chiefs of Staff, the top-ranking position in the armed forces. His service as a military adviser to President Ronald Reagan in the 1980s and other experience in international political affairs led Bush to name him secretary of state, and the Senate confirmed him on January 20, 2001.

In October 1989, U.S. secretary of defense Dick Cheney swears in Colin Powell as chairman of Joint Chiefs of Staff while Powell's wife holds the Bible.

On September 11, 2001, the Muslim terrorist group al Qaeda attacked the United States. Al Qaeda was based in Afghanistan, and Powell advised Bush on how to retaliate for the attack, which included invading Afghanistan on October 7, 2001. Powell also played a key role in starting the war against Iraq on March 20, 2003. Powell helped convince other nations that it was necessary for the United States to invade Iraq because it had weapons of mass destruction, such as missiles and poison gas, that posed a threat to the Middle East.

Powell made that argument on February 5, 2003, in a speech to the United Nations Security Council. Only two years earlier, however, Powell had claimed Iraq did not have such weapons.

Some historians believe Powell still did not think Iraq had such weapons but argued that it did out of loyalty to the president. Powell was quoted later as telling an aide before the invasion "I wonder what we'll do when we put half a million troops on the ground in Iraq and search it from one end to the other—and find nothing."[86] When no weapons were discovered, Powell and the Bush administration were accused of having twisted intelligence data to justify the invasion.

Rice was a Stanford University political science professor in 2000 when Bush made her his national security adviser. She was the first black woman to hold that position. Bush chose her to succeed Powell and the U.S. Senate confirmed her 85–13 on January 26, 2005. The thirteen negative votes were the most against

Condoleezza Rice and Terrorism

As secretary of state, Condoleezza Rice has battled Muslim terrorists. Rice first learned about the use of terror in Birmingham, Alabama, on September 15, 1963, when racist whites blew up the African American Sixteenth Street Baptist Church. Rice was a playmate of one of four children killed in the blast. Rice claims white terrorists failed that day to intimidate blacks from seeking their civil rights:

> I did not see it happen, but I heard it happen, and I felt it happen, just a few blocks away [and it] is a sound that I will never forget, that will forever reverberate in my ears. That bomb took the lives of four young girls, including my friend and playmate, Denise McNair. The crime was calculated to suck the hope out of young lives, bury aspirations and ensure that all fears would be propelled forward into the next generation. But those fears were not propelled forward, those terrorists failed. They failed because of the poverty of their vision, a vision of hate and inequality and the primacy of difference, and they failed because of the courage and sacrifice of all who suffered and struggled for civil rights.

Stan Correy, "Background Briefing: Condoleezza, Condoleezza," Australian Broadcasting Corporation, April 3, 2005. www.abc.net.au/rn/talks/bbing/stories/s1338813.html.

a secretary of state nominee since 1825. The senators voted no to show their lack of confidence in Rice, who like Powell had been criticized for making false claims about Iraqi weapons to justify war. Although some African Americans also dislike Rice because they oppose the Iraq War, others appreciate her as a role model. Michelle Moore is a senior vice president for the National Urban League, a black civil rights group. Moore claims, "Regardless of whether or not we agree on positions that Condoleezza Rice has taken on issues and policies does not diminish the fact that she is a history-making figure. She continues to push the boundaries of opportunity for African American women. We may not agree on everything, but that's okay."[87]

Much of the negative reaction to Rice's performance as secretary of state was due to the unpopularity of the Iraq War. However, most black appointed officials throughout history have been honored for accomplishing so much despite the handicaps they faced due to racism.

Many Black Officials

Black appointed officials today are accustomed to working in nearly every job at every level of government. However, it has not always been easy for the first blacks named to particular positions to do their jobs. Edward R. Dudley, who in 1949 was named ambassador to Liberia, has admitted that it was hard being the first U.S. black ambassador: "It was not easy to lead the way back in those days. I hope I made a small contribution."[88] Dudley not only had to learn to handle a new job but perform extremely well so other blacks could have the same opportunity. In 1965 Harris became the first black female ambassador when she was posted to Luxembourg.

For Iowa educator W. Ray Richardson, being "the first black" was a common experience. Richardson in March 2002 was named superintendent of the Ames Community School District to become the first African American to head an Iowa local school system. Richardson has said he was proud of establishing so many "firsts" as a teacher, principal, and district head: "I can't ignore it, and I don't want to ignore it. I have been the first a lot in my career. But, at the same time, I've worked hard to get noticed by virtue of my abilities and skills. I didn't get the job because I was black."[89]

Richardson earned his position with decades of hard work in his profession. So did Bill Clay, who in February 2007 was named police chief in Belleville, Illinois. Clay was the first black the city had hired a dozen years earlier after the federal government ordered it to integrate its police department. Clay had excelled as an officer since then. When mayor Mark Eckert chose him as police chief, he said "I'm not appointing Bill Clay to create history. In my eyes, Bill Clay is a professional."[90]

When blacks are the first ones to hold important posts, their performance is often heavily scrutinized by whites. This has been especially true in southern states where some whites still resent black officials. During the 1960s the white police in Selma, Alabama, brutally treated black civil rights protesters. In 1997 when Earnest Tate became the city's first black police chief, he said, "I want to be fair to the white and Black."[91] Even though Tate had been on the force for thirty years, he knew whites would be watching closely to see if he would favor blacks or discriminate against whites.

"The Ultimate Champion"

Perhaps no black official has ever been more revered than Thurgood Marshall. When he retired from the Supreme Court on June 28, 1991, U.S. representative Eleanor Holmes Norton of the District of Columbia noted that blacks honor him as much for ending school segregation as being the first black justice. Norton said: "He was, for us, the ultimate champion. It was largely his influence that made peaceful the route the equal rights struggle for blacks took. The *Brown* decision was the watershed moment for black Americans."[92]

Epilogue

Black Officials Still Face Racism

No black officials served in the United States for most of its existence. In 1904 the *Florida Times-Union* newspaper wrote that "in the South, the negro in politics is not tolerated" and claimed, "If the negro be wise, he will respect the limits set for him as does the elephant and the tiger and the others who accept rules and make no pretense to reason."[93] The newspaper's mocking tone equated blacks with wild animals and declared whites would not allow them to vote or hold office. Once blacks regained their right to vote in the 1960s, they not only proved themselves qualified voters but able government officials. This was especially true in the South, where whites for several centuries had either forced blacks into slavery or denied them basic rights. In 2000, Mississippi and Alabama combined had more black elected officials—1,628—than there were in 1970 in the entire nation—1,469.

Despite the gains blacks have made in recent decades, discrimination continues to negatively affect their lives. In his 2007 biography Brooke, the first black elected to the U.S. Senate, wrote, "We have made progress on civil rights but so much remains undone. [The promise] of the American dream continues to be far from its reality for millions of our citizens."[94] This is true even for black officials.

Officials Not Immune to Racism

White law enforcement officials and security guards sometimes treat blacks more harshly than they do whites. This even happens to prominent black officials like former Virginia governor Wilder. In March 1995, one year after Wilder's term as governor ended, he traveled to North Carolina to speak at Duke University. At the Raleigh-Durham Airport for his return flight home, Wilder was roughed up by a white security guard after he triggered an airport metal detector. Wilder described what happened: "When I told the white security man that it must be my suspenders [that set off the detector], he literally snapped. He grabbed me, then pushed me and choked me. [It] shouldn't make any difference whether I am a former governor. A human being shouldn't be treated this way."[95]

On March 29, 2006, U.S. representative Cynthia McKinney of Georgia was involved in a more publicized incident when a white guard tried to stop her from entering the Capitol. McKinney hit the guard when he grabbed her. Although McKinney was criticized for striking the guard, she claimed, "The whole incident was instigated by the inappropriate touching and stopping of me—a female, black congresswoman."[96] Even though McKinney was not wearing a special pin the 435 members of the House use to identify themselves, she said the guard treated her more roughly than the circumstances warranted because she was black.

Some black officials claim they are singled out for attacks over minor political matters. California state legislators give their supporters replica Assembly badges. In December 2006 when Assemblyman Mervyn Dymally was criticized for abusing that practice, he claimed he was being politically attacked because of his race. Dymally, the state's first black lieutenant governor, said, "It's nice and proper and polite to say that racism doesn't exist in American society and politics. But it exists. People have to deal with that. Why am I being singled out?"[97]

Racists often threaten black officials with violence. This happens so often that some people were suspicious when the December 30, 2006, shooting death of mayor-elect Gerald Washington of Westlake, Louisiana, was ruled a suicide. Even though evidence indicated Washington shot himself, there was speculation a white person killed him because he did not want a black mayor. Terry

Welke is the Calcasieu Parish coroner who ruled Washington's death a suicide. Even Welke admitted that "this is the South, so of course everybody's going to say it was some white guy shooting a black guy."[98]

Such incidents show that some whites still hate or fear the thought of black officials. This sort of racism surfaced in 2007 after U.S. senator Barack Obama announced he was running for president.

Violence and Barack Obama

The U.S. Secret Service had to begin protecting Obama in May 2007 because of threats made against him on white supremacist Web sites and in letters he received. One racist blogger wrote, "Our world will become unbearable with him as president. Maybe there will be someone who would take [a] chance and do a Lincoln on him? Is that our only hope?"[99] Abraham Lincoln was the first U.S. president to be assassinated, and the posting was considered a death threat. That and other threats of violence forced the government to provide security for Obama and his family earlier in a campaign than for any candidate who ever ran for president.

Racism is also evident in some criticism of Obama. Opponents have raised concerns about whether the first-term senator has enough experience to be president; such criticism is acceptable in a political campaign. Some whites, however, oppose Obama because they believe no black is competent to be president. When such people attack Obama's positions on issues or statements he has made, they often use racist terms, obscenities, and other offensive language.

That became a problem for the CBS television network, which allowed people to post comments about stories it ran on presidential candidates on CBSNews.com, its Web site. On May 4, 2007, Mike Sims, director of news and operations for CBSNews.com, said the network would no longer accept postings for Obama stories because so many comments were offensive. Said Sims: "It's very simple. [CBS does not allow] personal attacks, especially racist attacks. Stories about Obama have been problematic, and we won't tolerate it."[100] Sims said editors usually trimmed such offensive language but that it was impossible with the Obama stories because there were so many objectionable comments.

The negative reaction to Obama shows how much some whites disagree with the claim he made on July 27, 2004, in his keynote speech to the Democratic National Convention. Obama declared, "There's not a black America and white America and Latino America and Asian America—there's the *United States* of America. We are one people."[101] Racist comments against Obama show that race still divides the nation.

The Pride of Black Officials

The difficulties blacks encounter due to racism make them all the more joyous when they do become public officials. On November 19, 2007, the nearly all-white Mequon-Thiensville School District in Wisconsin unanimously chose Demond Means as its superintendent, making him one of nearly 330 blacks to head local school districts. Afterward Means said, "There's an old [African] saying, 'I am hyena happy and peacock proud' to be the next superintendent."[102] And that is a feeling that has been shared by every other black official throughout U.S. history.

Notes

Introduction: From Slavery to Public Office

1. Barack Obama, "The Text of Barack Obama's Keynote Address to the 2004 Democratic National Convention," PBS, July 27, 2004. www.pbs.org/newshour/vote2004/demconvention/speeches/obama.html.

2. Obama, "The Text of Barack Obama's Keynote Address."

3. Quoted in Nell Irvin Painter, *Creating Black Americans: African-American History and Its Meanings, 1619 to the Present*. New York: Oxford University Press, 2006, p. 136.

4. Quoted in James Ragland, James Ragland column, *Dallas Morning News*, June 27, 2007, p. A1.

Chapter One: The First Black Political Officials

5. John Mercer Langston, *Freedom and Citizenship: Selected Lectures and Addresses of Hon. John Mercer Langston, LL.D., U.S. Minister Resident at Haiti*. Miami: Mnemosyne, 1969, pp. 98–99.

6. Quoted in Anne Wallace, "Famous Black Man Remains Enigmatic," *Times Union Albany, (NY)*, March 14, 1999, p. A4.

7. Quoted in Danielle Alexander, "Forty Acres and a Mule, the Ruined Hope of Reconstruction," *Humanities*, January/February 2004. www.neh.gov/news/humanities/2004-01/reconstruction.html.

8. Quoted in Foster Rhea Dulles, *The United States Since 1865*. Ann Arbor: University of Michigan Press, 1971, p. 25.

9. Quoted in Dorothy Sterling, ed., *The Trouble They Seen: Black People Tell the Story of Reconstruction*. New York: Doubleday, 1976, p. 128.

10. Quoted in Eric Foner, *Forever Free: The Story of Emancipation and Reconstruction*. New York: Knopf, 2005, p. 128.

11. Quoted in Sterling, *The Trouble They Seen*, p. 190.

12. Quoted in Foner, *Forever Free*, p. 269.

13. Edward W. Brooke, *Bridging the Divide: My Life*. New Brunswick, NJ: Rutgers University Press, 2007, p. 148.

14. Quoted in William L. Clay Sr., *Just Permanent Interests: Black Americans in Congress, 1870–1991*. New York: Amistad, 1992, p. 17.

15. Quoted in James Haskins, *Distinguished African American Political and Governmental Leaders*. Phoenix: Oryx, 1999, p. 32.

16. Quoted in Dorothy Schneider and Carl J. Schneider, *An Eyewitness History: Slavery in America from Colonial Times to the Civil War*. New York: Facts On File, 2000, p. 340.

17. Quoted in Robert Smalls Foundation, "Robert Smalls Timeline." www.robertsmalls.org/timeline.html.

Chapter Two: Blacks Lose, Then Regain, Political Power

18. Quoted in Chandler Davidson and Bernard Grofman, eds., *Quiet Revolution in the South: The Impact of the Voting Rights Act, 1865–1900*. Princeton, NJ: Princeton University Press, 1994, p. 192.

19. Quoted in Brian Steel Wills, *A Battle from the Start: The Life of Nathan Bedford Forrest*. New York: HarperCollins, 1992, p. 345.

20. Quoted in Sterling, *The Trouble They Seen*, p. 374.

21. Quoted in Foner, *Forever Free*, p. 135.

22. Quoted in Avery Craven, *Reconstruction: The Ending of the Civil War*. New York: Holt, Rinehart and Winston, 1969, p. 140.

23. Quoted in William Loren Katz, *Eyewitness: The Negro in American History*. New York: Pittman, 1971, p. 252.

24. Quoted in Eric Foner, *Reconstruction: America's Unfinished Revolution 1863–1877*. New York: Harper & Row, 1989, p. 582.

25. Quoted in Sterling, *The Trouble They Seen*, p. 477.

26. Quoted in Davidson and Grofman, *Quiet Revolution in the South*, p. 68.

27. Quoted in David S. Cecelski and Timothy B. Tyson, eds., *Democracy Betrayed: The Wilmington Race Riot of 1898 and Its Legacy*. Chapel Hill: University of North Carolina Press, 1998, p. 3.

28. Quoted in Quintard Taylor, *In Search of the Racial Frontier: African Americans in the American West, 1528–1990*. New York: Norton, 1998, p. 145.

29. Quoted in Janae Hoffler, "Voting Rights Took Years," *Philadelphia Tribune*, January 14, 2007, p. G3.

30. Lyndon Baines Johnson, "We Shall Overcome," speech delivered to a joint session of Congress on March 15, 1965. www.americanrhetoric.com/speeches/lbjweshallovercome.html.

Chapter Three: Blacks Govern Their Hometowns

31. Quoted in Thomas E. Cavanagh and Denise Stockton, *Black Elected Officials and Their Constituencies*. Washington, DC: Joint Center for Political Studies, 1983, p. 1.

32. Quoted in Florestine Purnell, Lori Rozsam, and Nancy Wilstach, "Bridge Builder," *People*, November 6, 2000, p. 75.

33. Quoted in David Firestone, "Making History at the Polls, Selma Elects a Black Mayor," *New York Times*, September 13, 2000, p. A20.

34. Quoted in Purnell, Rozsam, and Wilstach, "Bridge Builder," p. 75.

35. Quoted in Haskins, *Distinguished African American Political and Governmental Leaders*, p. 88.

36. Quoted in David R. Colburn and Jeffrey S. Adler, eds., *African-American Mayors: Race, Politics, and the American City*. Champaign: University of Illinois Press, 2001, p. 31.

37. Quoted in Emily Yellin, "Memphis Mayor Is Re-elected by a Surprisingly Wide Margin," *New York Times*, October 9, 1999, p. A12.

38. Quoted in *Time*, "In Other Political Developments," January 14, 1966, p. 36.

39. Quoted in Carl B. Stokes, *Promises of Power: A Political Autobiography*. New York: Simon & Schuster, 1973. p. 107.

40. Colburn and Adler, *African-American Mayors*, p. 1.

41. Quoted in J.E. White, "The Limits of Black Power," *Time*, May 11, 1992, p. 38.

42. Quoted in *Ebony*, "Alaska's First Black Mayor," October 1993, p. 64.

43. Quoted in LeGina Adams, "Look Who's Runnin' Things," *Black Enterprise*, July 2001, p. 26.

44. Quoted in Hans J. Massaquoi, "Introducing: Ron Kirk, First Black Mayor of Dallas," *Ebony*, September 1995, p. 32.

45. Quoted in Mellisa Blackburn, "Champion of Freedom," Metropolitan State College of Denver. www.mscd.edu/~themet/The Metropolitan/06_07/Vol29_issue19/metnews/noel.html.

46. Earl G. Graves, "Black Mayors Make a Difference," *Black Enterprise*, July 2001, p. 13.

Chapter Four: Blacks Govern Their States

47. Quoted in *Fort Lauderdale, (FL) Sun Sentinel*, "Success Story: Virginia Inaugurates Nation's First Black Elected Governor," January 14, 1990, p. A3.

48. Quoted in Illinois General Assembly Legislative Research Unit, "Cecil Partee Biography," *African American Legislators in Illinois*, February 2006, p. 22.

49. Quoted in *Richmond (VA) Times-Dispatch*, "Inaugural History," January 12, 1986, p. A22.

50. Quoted in Craig Hines, "Wilder Dismisses Race as Issue in Virginia," *Houston Chronicle*, November 9, 1989, p. 1.

51. Quoted in *Salt Lake Tribune*, "Yes, Virginia, Wilder Is Out of '92 Chase," January 9, 1992, p. A3.

52. Quoted in Bonnie V. Winston, "On His Last Day, Wilder Returns to His Roots and Warm Embraces," *Norfolk Virginian-Pilot*, January 15, 1994, p. D6.

53. Quoted in Michael Paulson, "'Answered Prayer'—1,000 Greet Patrick, Hail Step Forward in Struggle of Blacks," *Boston Globe*, January 3, 2007, p. B1.

54. Quoted in Casey Ross, "Gov's MLK Message: Let's Tackle Racism," *Boston Herald*, January 16, 2007, p. 6.

55. Quoted in John F. Guess Jr., "Polly Williams," *Headway*, September/October 1998, p. 18.

56. Quoted in Ed Vogel, "Election Victories: Black Legislators Overcome Odds," *Las Vegas Review-Journal*, December 23, 2002, p. 1.

57. Quoted in Aurelio Rojas, "Veteran Lawmaker Renews Black Caucus: With Dymally at the Helm, Group Could Grow to Record Number After Fall Election," *Sacramento (CA) Bee*, June 19, 2006, p. 1.

58. Quoted in Ovetta Wiggins, "Brown's Role Is Ambiguous. His Goal Isn't. Lieutenant Governor Keeps Service as Aim," *Washington Post*, April 30, 2007, p. B1.

59. Quoted in Monica Potts, "Treasurer Calls Affordable Housing a 'Moral Imperative,'" *Advocate*, November 16, 2007, p. A11.

60. Quoted in Haskins, *Distinguished African American Political and Governmental Leaders*, p. 259.

Chapter Five: Blacks Write Laws for the Entire Nation

61. *National Journal*, "In His Own Words: Excerpts from an October 30 Interview with House Ways and Means Committee Chairman Charles Rangel, D-N.Y," November 3, 2007, p. 27.

62. Quoted in Prem Thottumkara, "Oscar Stanton De Priest: Fighting 'Jim Crow' Inside the United States Congress," *Illinois History: A Magazine for Young People*, January 2007, p. 48.

63. Quoted in Clay, *Just Permanent Interests*, p. 80.

64. Quoted in Ed Davis, "Black Power Grows in Congress," *New Pittsburgh Courier*, November 7, 1992, p. A1.

65. Quoted in Elton C. Fax, *Contemporary Black Leaders*. New York: Dodd, Mead, 1970, p. 190.

66. Quoted in Kenneth J. Cooper, "First Black U.S. Senator Elected by Popular Vote Tells His Story," *Crisis*, January/February 2007, p. 47.

67. Quoted in Lisa Jones Townsel, "Sisters in Congress Prove They Have What It Takes to Bring About Change," *Ebony*, March 1997, p. 28.

68. Quoted in James Baron, "Shirley Chisholm, 'Unbossed' Pioneer in Congress, Is Dead at 80," *New York Times*, January 3, 2005, p. 1.

69. Quoted in Shola Lynch, "Shirley Chisholm Fought the Good Fight," *Crisis*, January/February 2005, p. 58.

70. Quoted in Eric L. Smith, "Changing of the Guard," *Black Enterprise*, January 1999, p. 17.

71. Quoted in Michael Riley, "Nixing Dixie," *Time*, August 2, 1993, p. 30.

72. Quoted in Noam Schreiber, "Race Against History," *New Republic*, May 31, 2004, p. 22.

73. Quoted in Deirdre Shesgreen, "African Americans in Congress Have Come a Long Way from 1965," *St. Louis Post-Dispatch*, February 26, 2007, p. 1

74. Quoted in Richard E. Cohen, "Rangel's Reach," *National Journal*, November 3, 2007, p. 24.

75. John Conyers, "Editorial," *USA Today*, January 4, 2008, p. A8.

76. Quoted in Barbara Charline Jordan, "Statement on the Articles of Impeachment," speech delivered to the House Judiciary Committee, July 25, 1974. www.americanrhetoric. com/speeches/barbarajordanjudiciary statement.html.

Chapter Six: Black Appointed Officials Also Govern

77. Quoted in Antonia Felix, *Condi: The Condoleeza Rice Story*. New York: Pocket Books, 2002, p. 1.

78. Quoted in Charlotte Snow, "Thurgood Marshall: A Better Angel," *Human Rights: Journal of the Section of Individual Rights & Responsibilities*, Summer 1992, p. 26.

79. Quoted in Justin Ewers, "Making History," *U.S. News & World Report*, March 22, 2004, p. 76.

80. Quoted in *Ebony*, "The Legacy of Thurgood Marshall 1908–1993," March 1993, p. 126.

81. Quoted in *Jet*, "First Black Federal Judge James B. Parsons, 81, Dies," July 5, 1993, p. 6.

82. Quoted in Katheryn Hayes Tucker, "Making History," *Georgia Trend*, June 2005, p. 20.

83. Quoted in James Barron, "Robert C. Weaver, 89, First Black Cabinet Member, Dies," *New York Times*, July 19, 1997, p. 1.

84. Quoted in *Jet*, "First Black Labor Secretary Alexis Herman Recalls She Learned Perseverance from Her Father," May 26, 1997, p. 5.

85. Quoted in *Jet*, "Highlights of Blacks and the Clinton Years 1992–2001—Bill Clinton," February 5, 2001, p. 1.

86. Quoted in "The Most Explosive Book of the Fall," *Esquire*, October 2006, p. 183.

87. Quoted in Michael H. Cottman and Anne Gearan, "Love Her or Leave Her, Condi Rice Still Does Black Women Proud," BlackAmericaWeb.

com, February 9, 2005. www.black americaweb.com/site.aspx/bawnews/condirice210.

88. Quoted in *Jet*, "Diplomats Laud First Black U.S. Ambassador, Edward R. Dudley," June 20, 1994, p. 6.

89. Quoted in Karla Scoon Reid, "An Iowa First: Being the 'First' Is a Common Experience for W. Ray Richardson," *Education Week*, April 24, 2002, p. 8.

90. Quoted in Lisa P. White, "Clay First African-American Hired After Federal Lawsuit," *News-Democrat* (Belleville, IL), February 21, 2007, p. 1.

91. Quoted in *Jet*, "Earnest Tate Named First Black Police Chief in Selma, AL," December 22, 1997, p. 22.

92. Quoted in Charlotte Snow, "Human Rights: Journal of the Section of Individual Rights & Responsibilities," Summer 1992, p. 29.

Epilogue: Black Officials Still Face Racism

93. Quoted in Payne and Green, *Time Longer than Rope*, p. 414.

94. Quoted in Brooke, *Bridging the Divide*, p. 1.

95. Quoted in Hans J. Massaquoi, "The New Racism," *Ebony*, August 1996, p. 56.

96. Quoted in Bob Kemper, "McKinney Accuses Capitol Hill Cop of Racism," *Atlanta Journal-Constitution*, April 1, 2006, p. A1.

97. Quoted in Jim Sanders, "Dymally: Race Is a Factor in Badge Dispute," *Sacramento (CA) Bee*, December 14, 2006, p. 1.

98. Quoted in Doug Simpson, "New Mayor's Death Sparks Dispute; Louisiana Officials Ruled It a Suicide, but Some Said Cops Are Covering Up a Murder," *Orlando (FL) Sentinel*, January 6, 2007, p. A15.

99. Quoted in Alex Spillius, "Obama Gets Protection; Secret Service Guards Him amid Fears of Plot," *Gazette* (Montreal, Quebec), May 5, 2007, p. A19.

100. Quoted in Brian Montopoli, "CBSNews.com Turns Off Comments on Obama Stories," May 4, 2007. www.cbsnews.com/blogs/2007/05/04/publiceye/entry2761854.shtml.

101. Quoted in David Mendell, *Obama: From Promise to Power*. New York: Amistad, 2007, p. 3.

102. Quoted in Lawrence Sussman, "Riverside Grad to Lead Mequon-Thiensville Schools," *Milwaukee Journal Sentinel*, November 20, 2007, p. B5.

Chronology

September 6th, 1836
Alexander Twilight is the first African American elected to public office and to a state legislature, the Vermont General Assembly.

April 2, 1855
John Mercer Langston is elected town clerk in Brownhelm, Ohio.

April 1868
Oscar Dunn (Louisiana) is the first African American elected lieutenant governor.

November 3, 1868
John Willis Menard of Louisiana is the first black elected to Congress but not allowed to serve.

February 25, 1870
Hiram R. Revels of Mississippi becomes the first African American to serve in the U.S. Senate.

December 12, 1870
Joseph Rainey of South Carolina is the first African American to serve in the U.S. House of Representatives.

December 9, 1872
P.B.S. (Pinckney Benton Stewart) Pinchback of Louisiana becomes the first African American governor.

November 6, 1928
Oscar Stanton De Priest of Illinois is the first African American elected to the U.S. House of Representatives in the twentieth century.

1937
William H. Hastie is named to the U.S. District Court of the Virgin Islands to become the first black federal judge.

November 1938
Crystal Bird Fauset is elected to the Pennsylvania House of Representatives to become the first African American woman state legislator.

November 8, 1960
Otis M. Smith is elected auditor general of Michigan to become the first black to win a statewide election since Reconstruction.

January 18, 1966
President Lyndon B. Johnson names Robert C. Weaver secretary of the Department of Housing and Urban Development to become the first African American member of a president's cabinet.

November 8, 1966
Edward Brooke of Massachusetts is the first African American elected

to the U.S. Senate in the twentieth century and the first by popular vote.

August 30, 1967

Thurgood Marshall becomes the first African American U.S. Supreme Court justice.

November 7, 1967

Carl B. Stokes is elected mayor of Cleveland and Richard G. Hatcher mayor of Gary, Indiana, to become the first African American mayors of large cities.

November 5, 1968

Shirley Chisholm of New York becomes the first African American woman elected to the U.S. Congress.

October 1, 1989

General Colin Powell becomes the first African American chairman of the Joint Chiefs of Staff of the U.S. military.

November 2, 1989

Douglas Wilder of Virginia is the first African American elected governor.

January 20, 2001

Colin Powell becomes the first African American U.S. secretary of state.

January 26, 2005

Condoleezza Rice becomes the first African American woman U.S. secretary of state.

June 2008

Barack Obama becomes the first African American to become the presumptive nominee for the Democratic presidential nomination.

For More Information

Books

Herb Boyd, ed., *Autobiography of a People: Three Centuries of African-American History Told by Those Who Lived It*. New York: Doubleday, 2000. Includes firsthand accounts of what it was like for civil rights workers to battle racism.

Clayborne Carson et al., eds., *The Eyes on the Prize Civil Rights Reader: Documents, Speeches, and Firsthand Accounts from the Black Freedom Struggle, 1954–1990*. New York: Viking, 1991. This excellent collection contains information on what happened during the civil rights movement as well as why it happened.

Philip Dray, *At the Hands of Persons Unknown: The Lynching of Black America*. New York: Random House, 2002. A scholarly but readable history of the violence that whites used to deny blacks their rights from the end of Reconstruction to the 1960s.

Karen Dudley, *Great African Americans in Government*. New York: Crabtree, 1997. For the younger reader, the book includes biographies of black officials like Shirley Chisholm, Adam Clayton Powell Jr., L. Douglas Wilder, and David Dinkins.

Eric Foner and Olivia Mahoney, *America's Reconstruction: People and Politics After the Civil War*. New York: HarperPerennial, 1995. A scholarly, informative treatment of this period.

Meg Greene, *Into the Land of Freedom: African Americans in Reconstruction*. Minneapolis: Lerner, 2004. A thorough study of the period for younger readers.

Web Sites

Black History Pages (www.blackhistory pages.com). This Web site has links to good Web sites on all aspects of African American history.

The Civil Rights Movement (www. ecsu.ctstateu.edu/depts/edu/text books/civilrights). A good list of many Web sites on the civil rights movement of the 1960s.

Civil War and Reconstruction (www. memory.loc.gov/learn/features/time line/civilwar/recon/reconone.html). This U.S. federal government Web site has images, documents, and first person accounts of Reconstruction.

Without Sanctuary (www.without sanctuary.org/main.html). This is the companion Web site to the book *Without Sanctuary: Lynching Photography in America*. It contains historical photographs and postcards, many of them shocking, plus information on the subject.

Index

Picture Credits

Cover: AP Images

AP Images, 38, 59, 74

© Bettmann/Corbis, 33, 42, 65, 76, 78

Charles Bonnay/Time Life Pictures/Getty Images, 40

© Corbis, 13, 17, 20, 22

© Corbis Sygma, 81

Fred De Van/Time & Life Pictures/Getty Images, 67

Kevin Dietsch/UPI/Landov, 62

Scott J. Ferrell/Congressional Quarterly/ Getty Images, 9

Cynthia Johnson/Time Life Pictures/Getty Images, 50

Joseph L. Murphy/UPI/Landov, 69

© North Wind Picture Archives, 18, 26, 29

Gail Oskin/WireImage/Getty Images, 55

Ben Rose/WireImage/Getty Images, 45

About the Author

Michael V. Uschan has written more than sixty books, including *Life of an American Soldier in Iraq*, for which he won the 2005 Council for Wisconsin Writers Juvenile Nonfiction Award. It was the second time he has won the award. Uschan began his career as a writer and editor with United Press International, a wire service that provided stories to newspapers, radio, and television. Journalism is sometimes called "history in a hurry." Uschan considers writing history books a natural extension of the skills he developed in his many years as a journalist. He and his wife, Barbara, reside in the Milwaukee suburb of Franklin, Wisconsin.